Table of Contents

THE LIVING MACHINE

The human body can be compared to an extraordinary machine, composed of about 100,000 billion cells. The harmonious functioning of these microscopic components is what enables us to move, to speak, to think, and to create.

As with a car, the functioning of an organism is based on the perfect organization of all of its parts. No single cell acts independently; each coordinates its behavior with the other cells, transmitting and receiving messages continuously. These messages are almost always in the form of chemical molecules, but some are also electrical impulses.

The cells of the human body are grouped in an orderly fashion at different levels of organization. Those cells whose functions are more closely related are gathered in the tissues, such as muscular, skeletal, or blood. Differ-

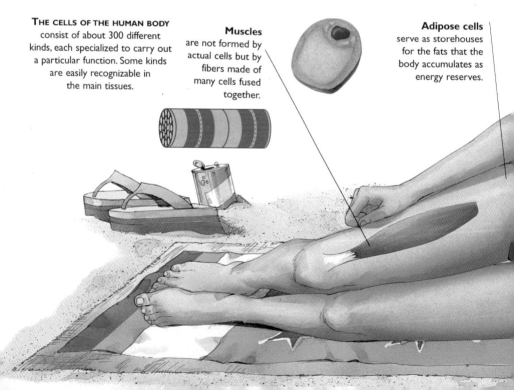

THE CELLS OF THE HUMAN BODY consist of about 300 different kinds, each specialized to carry out a particular function. Some kinds are easily recognizable in the main tissues.

Muscles are not formed by actual cells but by fibers made of many cells fused together.

Adipose cells serve as storehouses for the fats that the body accumulates as energy reserves.

THE HUMAN BODY
IN ACTION

EG31404

BARRON'S

DoGi

ent tissues form organs, analogous to the components of a car, such as the motor, the brakes, or the gas tank. Organs whose functions are highly related make up an organ system. For example, the mouth and the stomach are two different organs, but both are part of the digestive system, which includes all of the organs responsible for the digestion of food. The interactions among these complex organ systems carry out the functions of the entire human body. In this book, we will compare the organism to a machine. We will try to understand how the union of so many different parts

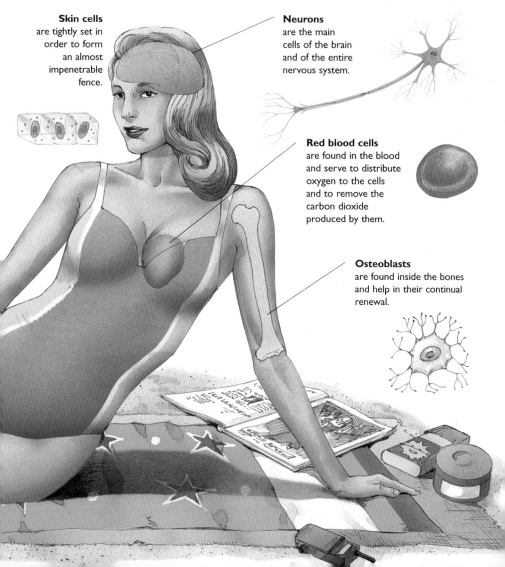

Skin cells are tightly set in order to form an almost impenetrable fence.

Neurons are the main cells of the brain and of the entire nervous system.

Red blood cells are found in the blood and serve to distribute oxygen to the cells and to remove the carbon dioxide produced by them.

Osteoblasts are found inside the bones and help in their continual renewal.

creates a single individual and what mechanism governs such relatively simple but vital functions as digestion or such highly complex ones as memory. We will then try to discover the small characteristics that make human beings so different from the other animals, which are also made up of cells, tissues, organs, and systems.

The cell and DNA: our instruction manual

Cells are nature's most extraordinary invention, the foundation of an animal's body and its source of life. All living things have their origins in a cell—in the case of humans, the male is developed from an egg fertilized by a sperm cell's (y) chromosome, and the female is formed when the egg is

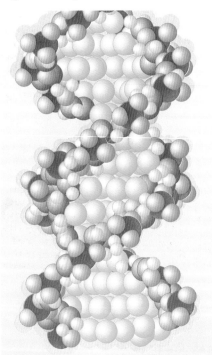

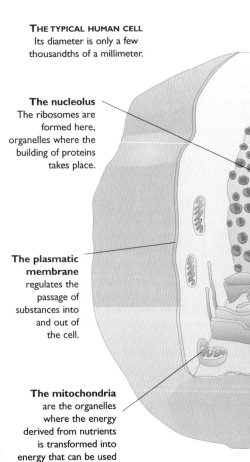

THE TYPICAL HUMAN CELL
Its diameter is only a few thousandths of a millimeter.

The nucleolus
The ribosomes are formed here, organelles where the building of proteins takes place.

The plasmatic membrane
regulates the passage of substances into and out of the cell.

DNA
has a three-dimensional structure formed by two interlaced spiral-shaped filaments. The figure shows a model in which each sphere corresponds to an atom. In reality, the DNA of a human cell is two-millionths of a millimeter in diameter and about 6$^{1}/_{2}$ feet (2 m) long. It is divided into about 100,000 small units, called genes, each of which contains information that is useful to the cell.

The mitochondria
are the organelles where the energy derived from nutrients is transformed into energy that can be used by the cell.

fertilized by a sperm cell's (x) chromosome.

Each cell is capable of carrying out "in miniature" the typical life functions for the entire organism. These functions include reproduction, growth, irritability, movement and locomotion, nutrition, and respiration. Some organisms, such as protozoans, amoeba, and paramecium, consist of a single cell.

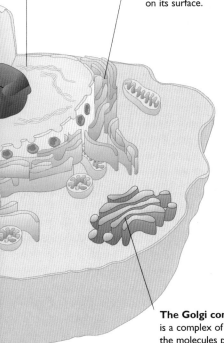

The nucleus
houses DNA
and is the
control center
for all of the
cell's activities.

**The endoplasmic
reticulum**
is a complex of
communicating
tubules and sacs. The
ribosomes are found
on its surface.

Occlusive junctions
hold the cells together
so closely that nothing
can pass between them.
For example, in blood
vessels, they prevent the
blood from escaping.

Settate junctions
contain several canals
that allow substances to
pass from one cell to
another. The canals
can open and close
following appropriate
signals.

The Golgi complex
is a complex of sacs where
the molecules produced by
the cell are developed and
stored.

Adherent junctions
are the loosest of all
junctions and keep the
cells joined by means of
fine filaments, allowing
substances to flow from
them.

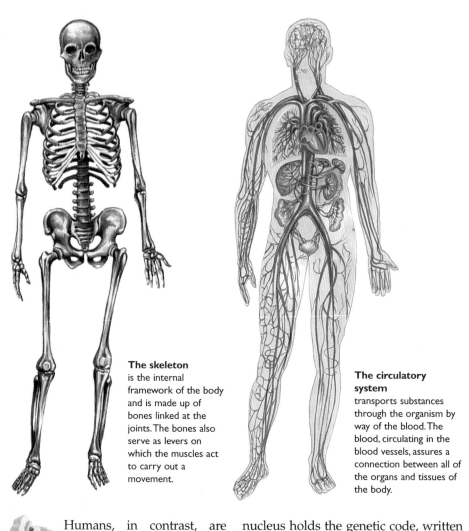

The skeleton is the internal framework of the body and is made up of bones linked at the joints. The bones also serve as levers on which the muscles act to carry out a movement.

The circulatory system transports substances through the organism by way of the blood. The blood, circulating in the blood vessels, assures a connection between all of the organs and tissues of the body.

Humans, in contrast, are made up of trillions of cells.

Most of the cells that form the body of an animal have a similar structure, with small variations according to their specific tasks. In general, each of our cells consists of two zones: the nucleus and the cytoplasm. The cytoplasm contains numerous organelles, each with a special function. The nucleus holds the genetic code, written in the molecule called DNA.

DNA contains genes, or the instructions necessary to carry out all of the functions of the cell, from protein building to reproduction. All of the body's cells also have an identical genetic code, although many of them are specialized in function.

This means that they have a specific

The muscles

enable the body to move and protect the internal organs. The latter are also often made of or covered by muscles that allow them to dilate or constrict.

The skin

is the body's external covering. It is impermeable and helps to maintain a constant internal body temperature, regardless of external variations. It creates an almost impenetrable barrier against viruses, bacteria, and other pathogenic organisms.

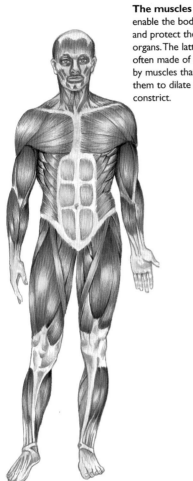

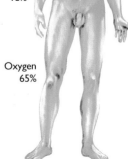

Other elements 1%

Phosphorus 1%

Calcium 2%

Nitrogen 3%

Hydrogen 10%

Carbon 18%

Oxygen 65%

task, and to carry it out, they utilize only certain pieces of information contained in their DNA. Consequently, the other pieces are never "read." This is why, in the same organism, we can find very different cells, even though all possess the same genetic code.

The main constituents of the human body are oxygen, hydrogen, and carbon (components of water, carbohydrates, and proteins). Proteins also contain nitrogen, while calcium is found in the bones and phosphorus in the blood and many other tissues.

THE QUEST FOR ENERGY

Like every machine, the human body needs energy in order to function. Energy enables the cells to carry out all life functions. These functions include synthesizing those molecules necessary for growth, repair, and reproduction.

The human body extracts the energy that it requires from food. However, a piece of bread or a slice of meat is made up of complex food particles. Such particles must pass through the digestive system before energy can be extracted from them. The digestion process changes complex food particles into simple ones. As a result, simple molecules such as sugars (glucose), amino acids, and fatty acids are produced. Only after food is digested can the cells extract the energy they need to carry out vital

THE IDEAL DIET
No single food contains all of the nutrients that an adult needs. Therefore, it is necessary to have a varied diet and to combine foods so as to take in the proper quantities of carbohydrates, proteins, fats, fiber, and vitamins.

Proteins can be obtained from meat, legumes, and cereals, which are also the main source of carbohydrates.

Fruit and vegetables contain sugars, vitamins, mineral salts, and fiber. The body cannot draw energy from them but they are still indispensable because their presence stimulates the movements of the intestines.

functions. These components are the right size to enter the cells, but they still contain too much energy.

The cells, then, are like a person who receives a large bill but must make many small purchases and so needs to break the bill into smaller denominations. For the cells, this energy "change" is a molecule called ATP. To obtain this molecule, the sugars, amino acids, and fatty acids—once they have entered the cytoplasm—are broken down into small chains made up of three carbon atoms. These atoms are then transferred to the mitochondria, where they are finally split and where the energy that

THE SENSATION OF HUNGER
is the result of the action of many different organs.

Fats
must be taken in moderation but are an important source of energy. They are found primarily in oil and butter.

Decrease in sugars
When the quantity of sugars in the blood decreases, the pancreas stops secreting insulin, the hormone that helps the sugars to enter into the cells.

The brain cells
don't have reserves of molecules from which to draw energy. Thus, they depend entirely on the nutrients carried by the blood. When these run short the effect is immediate and it becomes difficult to concentrate.

The vagal nerve
arouses a good part of the digestive tract. It is stimulated when the brain registers an insulin deficiency. In response the nerve causes an increase in salivation and the secretion of gastric juices in the stomach.

Milk
is one of the most complete sources of nutrition that exists; in fact, it contains fats, proteins, sugars, mineral salts, and vitamins.

THE DAILY NEED FOR ENERGY
Expressed in calories, it is different in each individual and depends primarily on the intensity of physical activity. The following examples refer to a man of about 30 years who weighs 145 pounds (66 kilos).

Sleeping, he consumes about 60 kilocalories per hour (Kcal/hour).

Studying or working at his desk, he consumes 170 Kcal/hour.

Gardening, or taking part in a moderate physical activity, he consumes 260 Kcal/hour.

Bicycling at 9.3 mph (15 kilometers per hour), he consumes 360 Kcal/hour.

they contain is distributed among many ATP molecules. The body needs oxygen for this process to occur. Oxygen is acquired through respiration, and the blood then transports it from the lungs to all of the cells. Without oxygen, the cells are not able to convert the energy contained in food into a usable form and are therefore condemned to die.

This is why no one can survive for more than a few minutes without breathing.

Breaking up food
The first phase of digestion occurs in the mouth, where food is broken into pieces so that it can be swallowed and sent to the stomach.

The task of breaking up and grinding every mouthful is done by the teeth.

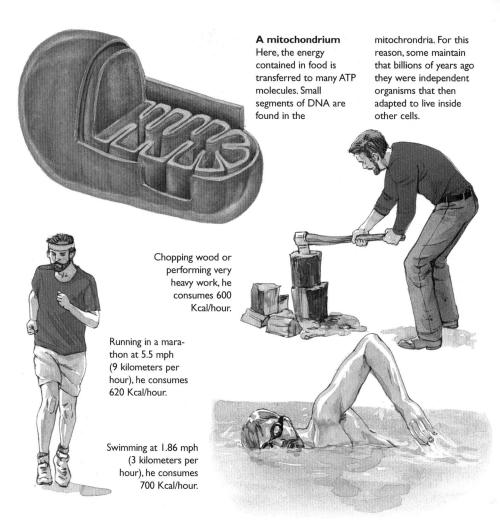

A mitochondrium
Here, the energy contained in food is transferred to many ATP molecules. Small segments of DNA are found in the mitochrondria. For this reason, some maintain that billions of years ago they were independent organisms that then adapted to live inside other cells.

Chopping wood or performing very heavy work, he consumes 600 Kcal/hour.

Running in a marathon at 5.5 mph (9 kilometers per hour), he consumes 620 Kcal/hour.

Swimming at 1.86 mph (3 kilometers per hour), he consumes 700 Kcal/hour.

The tongue, which has strong muscles, is used to keep the food in contact with the teeth and to mix it with saliva. Saliva is produced by three pairs of glands, located under the jaw, under the tongue, and in front of the ears. Saliva consists almost entirely of water and mucus, but also contains antibacterial antibodies and salivary amylase, a molecule that is capable of changing carbohydrates into starch. This first phase depends on the action of saliva, which plays a fundamental role in chewing. In fact, the mucus makes the food slippery or viscous, and able to slide into the esophagus during swallowing. Saliva, because it contains water, moistens the solid or dry substances as it aids in swallowing. In this way, food becomes softer and adheres

THE MOUTH
is the first part of the digestive tract. It is also fundamental for pronouncing sounds and contains certain zones of the immune system.

The maxillary (jaw) muscles
can clench the teeth with a force of up to 55 pounds (25 kilos) at the level of the incisors and 176 pounds (80 kilos) at the level of the molars.

The tonsils
produce cells responsible for defending the organism. They are located in the back part of the mouth, in a strategic position to impede possible viruses or bacteria that might penetrate the body through them.

The tongue and lips
are very important for articulating sounds. The taste buds on the tongue perceive flavors.

The teeth
An adult has 32, which differ according to their function. Molars grind; canines tear and rip; incisors pierce the food and cut it.

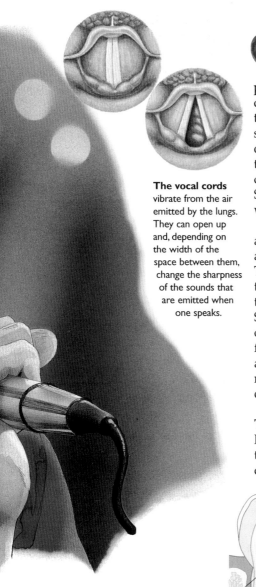

better to the taste buds that are embedded in the tongue.

Although saliva is more plentiful when we are eating, it is produced continuously. Calculations show that in 24 hours, 1.6 quarts (1.5 L) are secreted. In fact, saliva is required not only for chewing. It also protects the teeth because it contains antibodies and carries out a constant cleaning action. Saliva also keeps the oral cavity moist, which is essential for producing speech.

Once the food is mixed with saliva and stirred up with the tongue, it forms a ball, or bolus, ready to be swallowed. The tongue pushes the bolus toward the pharynx, where it will pass on to the esophagus and then to the stomach. Swallowing is a delicate process because the pharynx is also the pathway for air inhaled and sent to the trachea and then to the lungs. This pathway must not be blocked by food particles, or there is a risk of suffocation.

The stomach and intestines at work
Food that is swallowed is first stored in the stomach, where it is further broken down by the gastric juices. This organ

The vocal cords vibrate from the air emitted by the lungs. They can open up and, depending on the width of the space between them, change the sharpness of the sounds that are emitted when one speaks.

The enamel coats the teeth and is the hardest substance in the human body.

The pulp is the innermost layer of the tooth. Pulp contains nerves and blood vessels.

The dentine is the framework of each tooth and forms the roots that anchor it to the bone.

resembles a saddlebag and in an adult male has a storage capacity of about 1 quart. The stomach consists of muscle fibers, which enable it to stretch to an even greater volume.

The internal walls of the stomach are lined with many glands that secrete about 2 or 3 quarts (1.9–2.9 L) of gastric juices daily. These are made up of mucus, hydrochloric acid, and a protein called pepsinogen. When pepsinogen comes in contact with hydrochloric acid, it is transformed into pepsin, an enzyme molecule capable of breaking down the proteins in food. The tissues that make up the stomach, however, are also composed of many proteins and thus could also be attacked and literally digested by the pepsin. To prevent this, the mucus adheres to the stomach walls, forming a protective layer.

The food is partially digested in the

SATIETY
When the glucose circulating in the blood increases following food intake, the satiety center comes into play, inhibiting the hunger center.

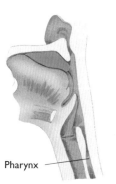
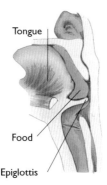
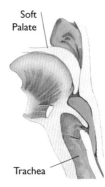

Tongue

Food

Pharynx

Epiglottis

Soft Palate

Trachea

Swallowing
The tongue pushes a mouthful of food toward the pharynx, and the soft palate rises, closing the pathway to the nose. Finally, descending along the pharynx, the mouthful lowers a membrane called the epiglottis, which closes the access to the trachea. In this way, the mouthful cannot block the respiratory path.

Gastric juices
The brain registers the sight of food, its taste, and its odor. This stimulates the stomach to secrete gastric juices.

The hunger center
Like the satiety center, it is found in the brain. The expansion of the stomach helps inhibit the feeling of hunger. The expansion is registered by certain nerves when the stomach receives food.

Carnivores
sink their teeth into the meat to rip and tear it. They have sharp teeth, like human canines.

Herbivores
They mash and grind the strong vegetable fibers; thus, their teeth are flat and wide, like human molars.

Rodents
They eat seeds, and therefore have strong and sharp teeth, similar to human incisors.

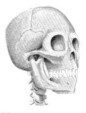

Humans
They are omnivores and have teeth of all shapes, in order to take nourishment from meat, seeds, or vegetables.

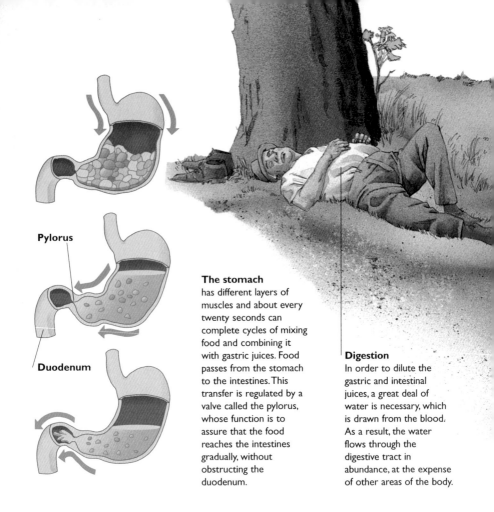

Pylorus

Duodenum

The stomach
has different layers of muscles and about every twenty seconds can complete cycles of mixing food and combining it with gastric juices. Food passes from the stomach to the intestines. This transfer is regulated by a valve called the pylorus, whose function is to assure that the food reaches the intestines gradually, without obstructing the duodenum.

Digestion
In order to dilute the gastric and intestinal juices, a great deal of water is necessary, which is drawn from the blood. As a result, the water flows through the digestive tract in abundance, at the expense of other areas of the body.

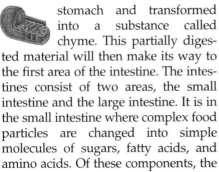 stomach and transformed into a substance called chyme. This partially digested material will then make its way to the first area of the intestine. The intestines consist of two areas, the small intestine and the large intestine. It is in the small intestine where complex food particles are changed into simple molecules of sugars, fatty acids, and amino acids. Of these components, the fats are the most difficult to break down. Because fats do not dissolve in water, enzymes are not able to break them down at this point. The digestion of fats, then, is not an immediate process. Another substance, bile, secreted by the liver, is needed to break the fats into smaller parts before digestion can begin. Emulsification of fats results in smaller fragments. The process is similar to the way a solvent acts on an oil

AFTER A MEAL
Like all of the other organs that
are not involved in digestion, the
brain receives less blood. Thus, the
nerve cells remove waste
products from their metabolism
with difficulty; they are less
efficient, and drowsiness sets in.

stain. These smaller fragments are more easily attacked by the pancreatic enzymes that are needed to convert fats into simple molecules of fatty acids. These fragments are more easily attacked by certain molecules produced in the pancreas, which completely break down the fats into simple fats.

Other enzymes, which come from the pancreas or are produced directly by the intestines, have the task of breaking down the proteins into amino acids, and the carbohydrates into sugars, such as glucose, fructose, or galactose.

Sugars and amino acids are absorbed into the walls of the small intestine, while fats must be washed by the lymph system before absorption can occur. The absorption process of the nutritive substances resembles the task of drying up a liquid with a sponge: the greater the surface of the sponge, the more quickly the operation is performed. For this reason, the internal surface of the small intestine is greatly increased by small finger-shaped folds called villi. If villi were laid out, they would cover an area the size of a tennis court. Whatever has not been absorbed, which is primarily water, salts, and undigested fiber, reaches the large intestine. Many microorganisms called bacteria live here. They have evolved in such a way as to live optimally with the human species. In exchange for the sustenance furnished by our bodies, they synthesize fundamental vitamins for us, such as vitamin K and vitamin B. When we undergo extended antibiotic treatments, the bacteria that make up the intestinal flora die. They may be replaced by bacteria that not only do not aid humans, but often cause serious illnesses.

The large intestine reabsorbs the water at the end of the digestion process. Each day, we drink about 1.5 quarts (1.5 L) of water directly. We also pour into the digestive tract about another 7 quarts (7 L) as liquid components of saliva, gastric and intestinal juices, or bile. The body retains most of the water; the feces contain on an average only 0.1 quart (0.1 L), in addition to a volume equivalent to 0.04 quart (0.05 L) of solids. The solids consist of mucus waste, dead cells from the intestines, bacteria, and indigestible food substances, such as vegetable fibers.

The last leg of the voyage
The substances absorbed by the digestive tract, with the exception of the long molecules of simple fats, pass into the

Hepatic lobules are the functional units of the liver. They receive the branches of the vena portae and the vena cava. Their cells purify the nutrients and accumulate sugars, in the form of glycogen, that are not immediately necessary.

The liver receives and sorts the nutrients absorbed by the intestines from the vena portae. The purified nutrients are then sent to the vena cava and depart for a journey in which they will resupply all of the cells of the body.

THE DIGESTIVE TRACT is made up of a tube about 33 feet (10 m) long that starts at the mouth and ends at the anus. Numerous glands and organs are connected to it, including the salivary glands, the liver, and the pancreas.

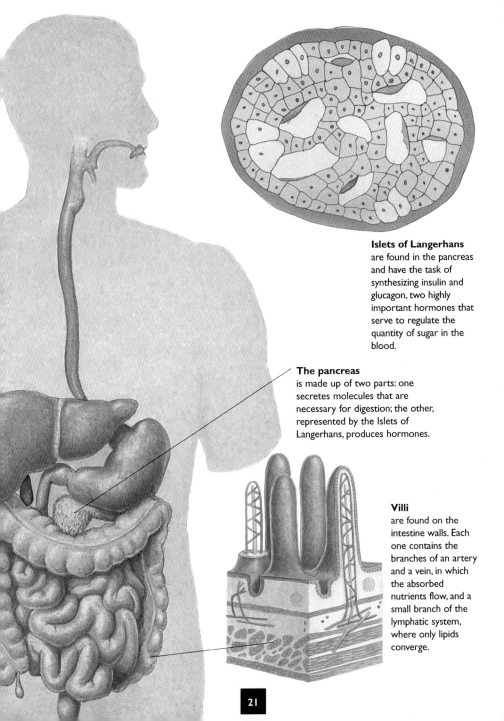

Islets of Langerhans
are found in the pancreas and have the task of synthesizing insulin and glucagon, two highly important hormones that serve to regulate the quantity of sugar in the blood.

The pancreas
is made up of two parts: one secretes molecules that are necessary for digestion; the other, represented by the Islets of Langerhans, produces hormones.

Villi
are found on the intestine walls. Each one contains the branches of an artery and a vein, in which the absorbed nutrients flow, and a small branch of the lymphatic system, where only lipids converge.

bloodstream. These nutrients are transported to the liver by the blood. The liver is the largest organ in the human body. In an adult it weighs about 3.3 pounds (1.5 kg). In addition to secreting bile, it has other extremely important functions. First, it is an inspection point where the food molecules are analyzed to eliminate those that are potentially harmful. Unfortunately, this control system is not infallible and sometimes certain toxic substances might enter an organism's tissue. At times, too, needed medications may be mistaken for harmful substances, and the liver may block the body from using them.

The liver is also a repository for energy reserves and stores sugars, in particular glucose. This happens because the cells are in constant need of small quantities of molecules from

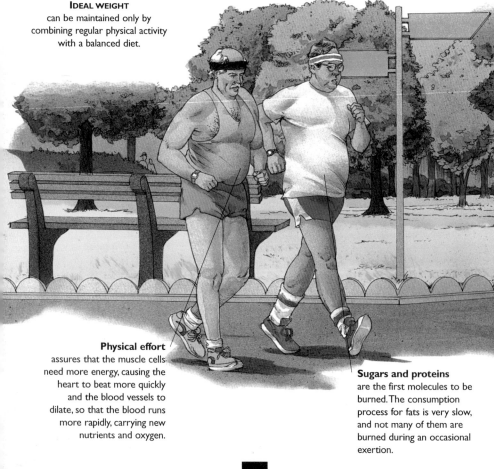

IDEAL WEIGHT
can be maintained only by combining regular physical activity with a balanced diet.

Physical effort
assures that the muscle cells need more energy, causing the heart to beat more quickly and the blood vessels to dilate, so that the blood runs more rapidly, carrying new nutrients and oxygen.

Sugars and proteins
are the first molecules to be burned. The consumption process for fats is very slow, and not many of them are burned during an occasional exertion.

which to draw energy. The cells themselves are unable to store energy except in very small amounts, so if excess molecules of nutrients were available, the energy would go to waste. As a result, the nutritive substances from food must be gradually introduced into the bloodstream, which carries them to each cell. Therefore, the glucose held by the liver is stored in the form of glycogen, a large molecule made up of a long chain of simple sugars. When the sugar level in the blood drops because the cells have removed all that is available, the liver breaks down the glycogen molecules and introduces them into the bloodstream. The concentration of glucose in the blood is controlled by the pancreas, which secretes two hormones —insulin and glucagon. The first stimulates the liver to produce glycogen and the second forces it to break it down.

Movement and heat
The sensation of heat that is perceived during physical activity is due to the fact that muscles in action heat up, just like a motor.

BREATHING
During physical activity, it is deeper and more frequent, in order for the muscles to receive more oxygen and to produce greater quantities of ATP.

Intercostal muscles
serve to increase the dilation capacity of the lungs. Under exertion a person needs more air than usual, and the increase in volume obtained by lowering the diaphragm is no longer sufficient.

Pulmonary capacity
In a normal breath, a person breathes about a pint of air. Under exertion it can reach as much as 3.5 quarts (3.5 L).

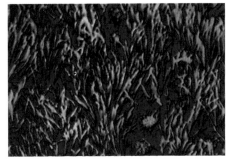

Purifying the air
The mucus that coats the trachea, bronchi, and bronchiole traps dust and infectious agents contained in the air that is inhaled. Subsequently, they are pushed toward the pharynx by "tentacles," called cilia, that belong to cells of the respiratory tract. From the pharynx, the mucus enters the digestive canal and is eliminated. Cigarette smoke has an anesthetic action on the cilia, hampering their activity.

How the body gets oxygen

As we have seen, the cells must convert the energy contained in food into ATP molecules. This conversion of ATP is carried out in a series of chemical reactions in which oxygen is consumed to make water and carbon dioxide is expelled. The process is continuous because the ATP "fuel" is burned and replaced without interruption (although the speed varies according to the intensity of the cellular activity). The cells constantly need new oxygen and nutrients and must eliminate carbon dioxide and waste molecules. Two systems work in harmony toward this end: the respiratory system and the circulatory system.

The respiration process is the task of drawing air from outside, taking in the oxygen, and substituting it with carbon dioxide. The lungs, two large sponge-

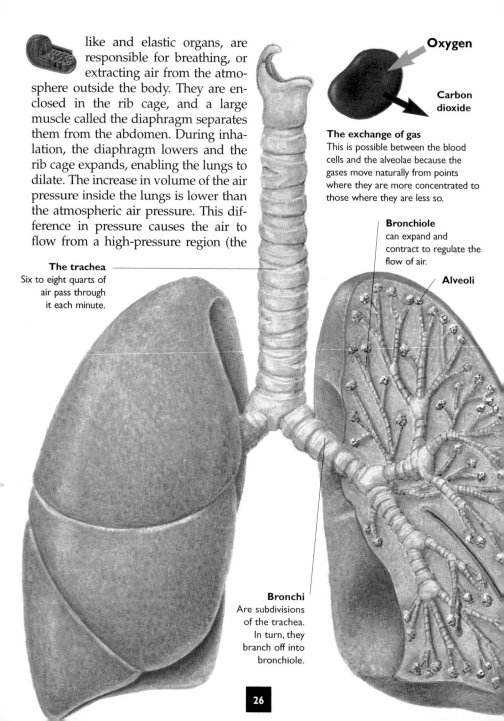

like and elastic organs, are responsible for breathing, or extracting air from the atmosphere outside the body. They are enclosed in the rib cage, and a large muscle called the diaphragm separates them from the abdomen. During inhalation, the diaphragm lowers and the rib cage expands, enabling the lungs to dilate. The increase in volume of the air pressure inside the lungs is lower than the atmospheric air pressure. This difference in pressure causes the air to flow from a high-pressure region (the

Oxygen

Carbon dioxide

The exchange of gas
This is possible between the blood cells and the alveolae because the gases move naturally from points where they are more concentrated to those where they are less so.

Bronchiole
can expand and contract to regulate the flow of air.

Alveoli

The trachea
Six to eight quarts of air pass through it each minute.

Bronchi
Are subdivisions of the trachea. In turn, they branch off into bronchiole.

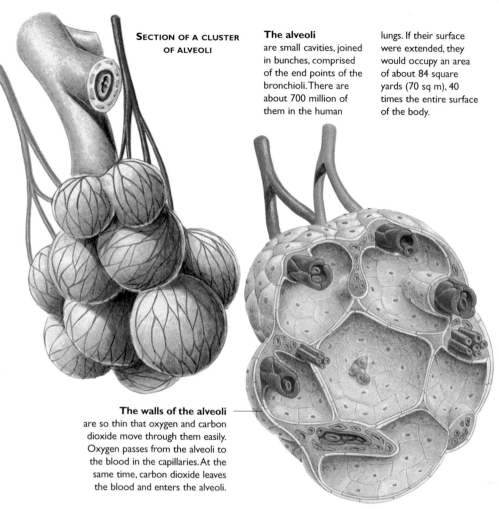

The alveoli are small cavities, joined in bunches, comprised of the end points of the bronchioli. There are about 700 million of them in the human lungs. If their surface were extended, they would occupy an area of about 84 square yards (70 sq m), 40 times the entire surface of the body.

The walls of the alveoli are so thin that oxygen and carbon dioxide move through them easily. Oxygen passes from the alveoli to the blood in the capillaries. At the same time, carbon dioxide leaves the blood and enters the alveoli.

atmosphere) to a low-pressure region (the lungs). From this, a brief lowering of the original pressure occurs, which is then restabilized when air enters. This new air reaches the lungs through the nose or the mouth and continues along the trachea and the bronchi. During the journey, it is heated and moistened. The cold, dry air that is normally in the external environment could damage the lungs.

The lungs contain an extremely intricate network of capillaries. The blood that runs through them has just completed a long journey, during which it has reached all of the body's cells, giving up oxygen and receiving carbon dioxide in return. Thus, the lungs function as a refueling station, in which the blood replenishes its load of oxygen and rids itself of carbon dioxide. When this exchange has taken place, exhala-

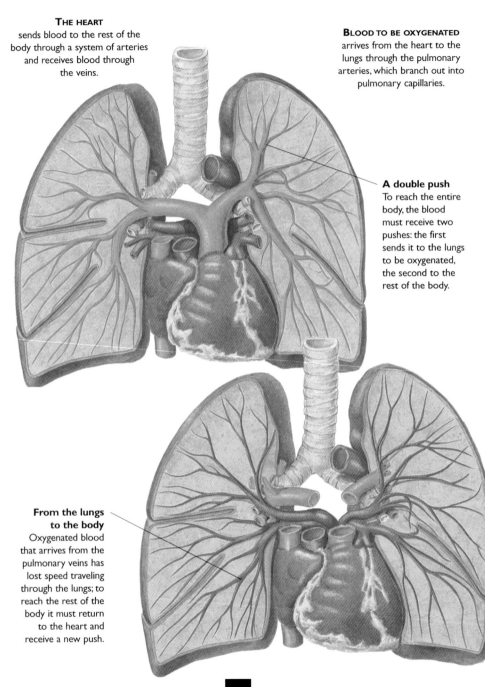

THE HEART
sends blood to the rest of the body through a system of arteries and receives blood through the veins.

BLOOD TO BE OXYGENATED
arrives from the heart to the lungs through the pulmonary arteries, which branch out into pulmonary capillaries.

A double push
To reach the entire body, the blood must receive two pushes: the first sends it to the lungs to be oxygenated, the second to the rest of the body.

From the lungs to the body
Oxygenated blood that arrives from the pulmonary veins has lost speed traveling through the lungs; to reach the rest of the body it must return to the heart and receive a new push.

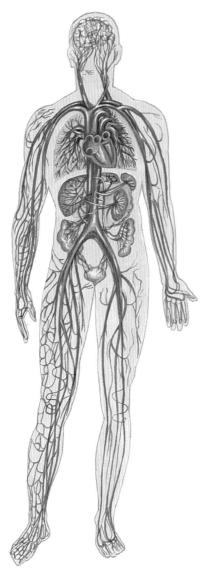

 tion begins: the diaphragm relaxes, causing a diminution in the volume of the rib cage. Thus, the air pressure in the lungs increases and, as a result, the lungs expel the air rich in carbon dioxide to the outside environment.

Circulation: a great system of connections

In order to live and "work," the 100,000 billion cells that make up the human body must continually receive food and oxygen and eliminate their waste. Moreover, the substances that some of these cells produce are destined to end up in other areas of the body, and so must be transported. It is not easy to satisfy the demands of so many "workers," and reaching them requires a highly efficient system of connections. The circulatory, or blood, system provides these connections. The system is a network of tubes, divided into arteries, capillaries, and veins, that together measure the incredible length of about 93,210 miles (150,000 km)—more than three times the circumference of the earth. Blood flowing through capillaries transports nutrient substances, as well as oxygen, into cells, while wastes, including carbon dioxide, are removed. The blood system is, in essence, an extremely long transporting band. Sometimes, enemies of the organism, such as viruses and bacteria, also use its flow to reach their targets.

The red blood cells are the most numerous cells in the blood. They are responsible for transporting oxygen and carbon dioxide. They are the only cells of the body to have lost their

From the tissues to the heart
Organs and tissues receive oxygenated blood from the arteries and send it to the heart by way of the veins. The speed of the blood slows down significantly in the tissues and veins. Before being able to run through the lungs' capillaries and be re-oxygenated, it first needs a new push.

nucleus. They are practically nothing more than small sacs filled with a molecule called hemoglobin, which can link itself either to oxygen or to carbon dioxide. In the first instance, the hemoglobin has a bright red color, which becomes dark red when it links itself to carbon dioxide. This is why one person's blood can appear to have different colors.

The other cells present in the blood are the white blood cells. There are different types of white blood cells. Each type is armed with its unique defense that will become activated if the body needs to fight off infection.

The blood flows through the circulatory system without interruption because of a very special muscle that functions as a pump: the heart. A healthy heart beats for a person's entire life without stopping or tiring: a comparable and continuous motion would be impossible, for example, with an arm muscle. This continuous heartbeat is due to unique characteristics of cardiac tissue, found only in the heart. In addition, and unlike other movements, the heartbeat is not the result of a

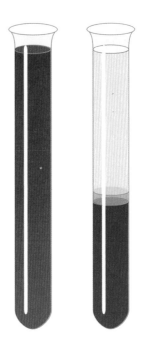

The blood is formed by a liquid part, plasma, and by different types of cells. If it is centrifuged, or spun rapidly, in a test tube, the heavier cells gather at the bottom while the plasma remains in the upper part.

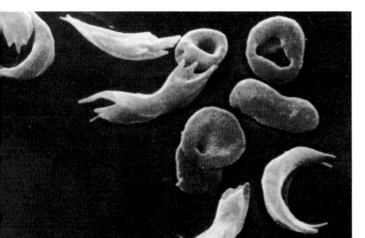

Sickle-cell anemia is a disease caused by a defect in the hemoglobin, the molecule that links oxygen from the lungs to the body tissues. As a result, this gas is no longer transported correctly; in addition, the red blood cells take on the shape of a sickle. Like many types of anemia, it is hereditary and can be fatal if the percentage of defective red blood cells is too high.

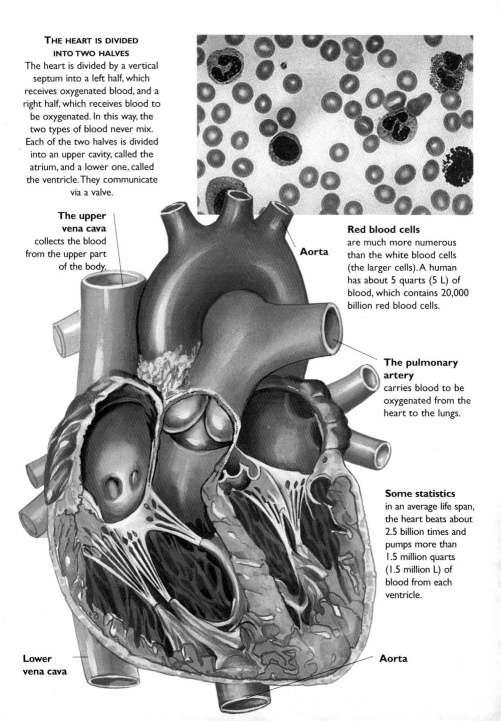

THE HEART IS DIVIDED INTO TWO HALVES

The heart is divided by a vertical septum into a left half, which receives oxygenated blood, and a right half, which receives blood to be oxygenated. In this way, the two types of blood never mix. Each of the two halves is divided into an upper cavity, called the atrium, and a lower one, called the ventricle. They communicate via a valve.

The upper vena cava collects the blood from the upper part of the body.

Aorta

Red blood cells are much more numerous than the white blood cells (the larger cells). A human has about 5 quarts (5 L) of blood, which contains 20,000 billion red blood cells.

The pulmonary artery carries blood to be oxygenated from the heart to the lungs.

Some statistics in an average life span, the heart beats about 2.5 billion times and pumps more than 1.5 million quarts (1.5 million L) of blood from each ventricle.

Lower vena cava

Aorta

response to a stimulus coming from the nervous system.

It is the heart itself that "sets the rhythm" to its own motion. Even if the heart were removed, it would continue to beat by itself for a short time. This unique self-beating characteristic in heart tissue makes heart transplants possible. Normally a heart beats about 70 times per minute. The overall control of the heartbeat is maintained through nerve impulses. The heartbeat will increase or slow down in response to the body's needs.

Maintaining internal equilibrium
Viewed from the outside, our body changes very slowly. It takes months or

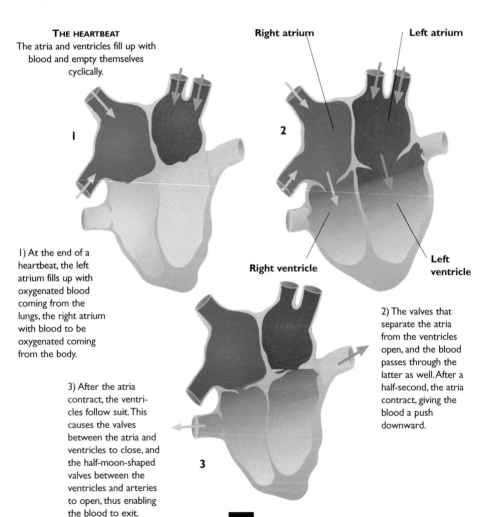

THE HEARTBEAT
The atria and ventricles fill up with blood and empty themselves cyclically.

Right atrium

Left atrium

1

2

Right ventricle

Left ventricle

1) At the end of a heartbeat, the left atrium fills up with oxygenated blood coming from the lungs, the right atrium with blood to be oxygenated coming from the body.

3) After the atria contract, the ventricles follow suit. This causes the valves between the atria and ventricles to close, and the half-moon-shaped valves between the ventricles and arteries to open, thus enabling the blood to exit.

3

2) The valves that separate the atria from the ventricles open, and the blood passes through the latter as well. After a half-second, the atria contract, giving the blood a push downward.

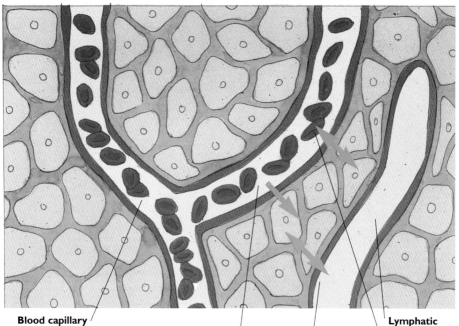

Blood capillary

Veins and arteries
Blood proceeds through the arteries (far left) thanks to the push from the heart. A push from the surrounding muscles is also necessary for the veins (left), and special valves prevent the blood from turning back.

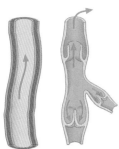

Water and substances such as nutrients pass through the tissues from the plasma.

Some of the water that is found in the cells travels to the lymphatic system, where it flows again into the blood.

Lymphatic capillary

The red blood cells yield oxygen to the tissues and receive carbon dioxide.

years before most changes become noticeable. The body's internal state also remains constant: the cells live in a stable environment, they are not subject to variations in temperature, and they receive a steady supply of the nutrients and oxygen they need to survive.

Such stability, which is called homeostasis, is not spontaneous but is achieved through a complex regulatory system. This assures that the cells do not function differently if we are at the North Pole or the Equator, or if we are fasting or feasting at a banquet. Because of these mechanisms of homeostasis, our physical aspect does not show change constantly, even though about 25 million cells are born every second. This is because an equal number of cells die and their remains, along with the

The kidneys are dark red in color and about 4 inches (10 cm) long.

Filtering the blood Each kidney receives blood, filters it, and eliminates waste products with urine.

Towards the bladder Urine is forced into canals through the urinary ducts and pushed toward the bladder by their contractions, which take place from one to five times per minute.

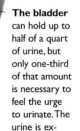

Eliminating waste When it leaves the bladder, the urine exits the body through a conduit called the urethra.

The bladder can hold up to half of a quart of urine, but only one-third of that amount is necessary to feel the urge to urinate. The urine is ex- pelled with a movement that is partly auto- matic and partly volun- tary: about 1.5 quarts are produced per day.

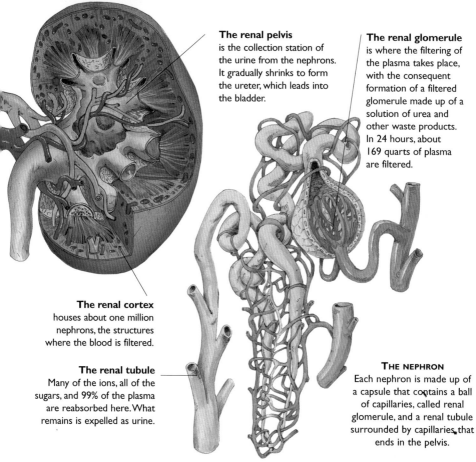

The renal pelvis
is the collection station of the urine from the nephrons. It gradually shrinks to form the ureter, which leads into the bladder.

The renal glomerule
is where the filtering of the plasma takes place, with the consequent formation of a filtered glomerule made up of a solution of urea and other waste products. In 24 hours, about 169 quarts of plasma are filtered.

The renal cortex
houses about one million nephrons, the structures where the blood is filtered.

The renal tubule
Many of the ions, all of the sugars, and 99% of the plasma are reabsorbed here. What remains is expelled as urine.

THE NEPHRON
Each nephron is made up of a capsule that contains a ball of capillaries, called renal glomerule, and a renal tubule surrounded by capillaries that ends in the pelvis.

waste produced by the normal activity of the other cells, is promptly eliminated.

We have already seen that lungs contribute to maintaining homeostasis by removing carbon dioxide from the body. The kidneys, however, also play a fundamental role in eliminating waste. The kidneys are two small, bean-shaped organs located in the rear portion of the abdomen, directly under the lower ribs.

The kidneys filter all of the body's blood several dozen times a day, removing toxic substances and wastes

that have flowed into it. These wastes include urea, a molecule produced during the breakdown of proteins.

Unlike fats and sugars, proteins cannot be stored as reserves in cells. When a human or other organism ingests excess protein, the liver breaks these molecules down. The breakdown process produces urea. Because urea is very toxic, it is quickly transported to the kidneys for immediate excretion.

The kidneys also take care of eliminating certain mineral salts from the plasma. Salts are fundamental elements

The hypothalamus
is the area of the brain that monitors the liquid component of the blood. This can become dangerously low when one has sweated a lot.

The thirst stimulus
is produced by the brain to replace lost liquids.

WHEN IT IS TOO HOT
the cells' metabolic activity slows down, in order to prevent the heat that the cells produce from being added to it. This can cause a sensation of apathy and fatigue.

Sweat
bathes the surface of the body and, as it evaporates, lowers its temperature.

The circulation
becomes more intense near the body's surface, because of the dilation of the superficial blood capillaries. The blood contained in the capillaries, running close to the skin, gives up its heat and cools, but its abundant presence makes the face and the extremities of the body turn red and swell.

 for survival of cells but can be harmful if an excess accumulates in the blood.

Urea and mineral salts, along with acids, hormones, excesses of certain vitamins, and even medicines, are the waste products that are eliminated by urine.

How quickly the kidneys clear urine depends on the amount of liquid con-sumed. The urine can be more plentiful if one has drunk a lot, and scarcer if one is dehydrated. The kidneys, however, have difficulty in removing excess salts. As a result, one cannot stop urinating even in the desert, nor can thirst be quenched with salt water. In fact, swallowing salt water would mean taking in additional salts, which would then require that the kidneys work

WHEN IT IS TOO COLD
If the body temperature seems at risk of being lowered, the hypothalamus sends signals to the rest of the body to stop the heat from being dispersed.

Producing more heat
The cells are pushed to increase their activity through two hormones: adrenaline and thyroxine.

Goose bumps
are caused by muscle contractions that make the skin tingle. It is a heritage of our past as hairy animals, when increasing the volume of hair served as insulation.

The blood vessels
The superficial blood capillaries contract when it is cold. This causes a reduction in the surface where the blood and skin come in contact, reducing the dispersion of body heat toward the outside to the minimum.

harder to eliminate the excess salt. An imbalance in salt intake might lead to dehydration, a condition that can be fatal.

Maintaining the body's homeostasis also assures constant internal body temperature. Our ideal temperature is between 98.6 and 98.8°F (36–37°C). A delicate balance is needed to regulate temperature and prevent it from increasing or decreasing as cells function. It is important that body temperature not exceed the ideal. Excess internal body heat prevents such cell activity as the synthesis of enzymes. Strenuous muscle activity is one thing that can trigger increased body temperature. The action of the hypothalamus prevents internal overheating.

COMMUNICATION AND COORDINATION

All the cells work to keep the entire organism alive and active. To do so, they must be coordinated. To this end, cells conduct a never-ending and extremely intense exchange of messages in our bodies.

Two systems are responsible for assuring effective communication within the body: the nervous system and the hormonal system.

The nervous system includes the brain and a network of nerves that extends to the most peripheral parts of the organism. The most important cells, the neurons, register stimuli from the external environment and the condition of the internal organs. With this information, the nervous system develops and communicates a response to those parts of the body that must react. The nervous system communicates through impulses that pass from one neuron to

Nervous stress can be influenced by hormonal stress. The brain under stress can also influence the pituitary gland, preventing the release of the hormones called gonadotropins.

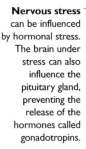

The "skipped" cycle The absence of gonadotropins has an impact on the ovaries. Ovulation is not stimulated without gonadotropins and therefore menstruation does not occur.

THE NERVOUS AND ENDOCRINE SYSTEMS are often influenced by events. For example, certain psychological situations can alter the menstrual flow.

another. The nervous system, then, has a rapid and direct means of communication, with few intermediaries.

The hormonal system is made up of specialized glands described as "ductless" because the glands pour their secretions directly into the bloodstream. The secretions are called hormones. Each functions as a chemical messenger, communicating directly with cells that must be able to interpret the message. Each hormone has a specific target cell.

Those cells that are not able to interpret the message let it pass by. However, when the hormones approach a cell that possesses a special molecule that enables it to recognize the message, they attach themselves to it and transmit their information. Hormones and

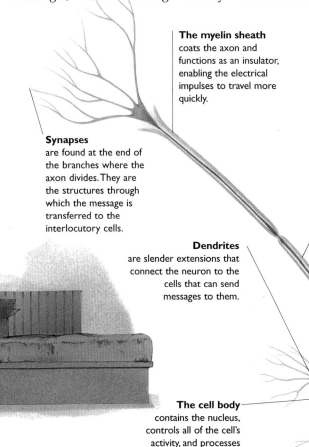

The myelin sheath coats the axon and functions as an insulator, enabling the electrical impulses to travel more quickly.

NEURONS have a very special structure, developed to optimally collect and transmit information.

The axon carries messages, in the form of electrical impulses. In humans, it can be up to 3.3 feet (1 m) long. Proportionately, if the cell body were the size of an orange, the axon would measure .9 mile (1.5 km).

Synapses are found at the end of the branches where the axon divides. They are the structures through which the message is transferred to the interlocutory cells.

Dendrites are slender extensions that connect the neuron to the cells that can send messages to them.

The cell body contains the nucleus, controls all of the cell's activity, and processes information collected by the dendrites.

receptors, then, are much like puzzle pieces. When the target cell has the right receptor, the hormone fits the surface much as two puzzle pieces fit together.

The specialist in short-distance communication: the neuron

Each type of body cell is a wonder and plays an important role in our survival. It would be impossible to live without skin, muscles, blood, or an immune system. The nervous system, though, has a particularly important role. Without this system, communication among vital organs could not exist.

It is the neurons' unique organization, as well as their activity, that enable us to think, imagine, and be conscious of what is happening around us. The biological secret that makes us particularly different from all other living things is hidden in our neurons.

Nevertheless, the structure of an isolated neuron is not particularly complicated. Even its way of transmitting messages is relatively simple and makes use of two tools: electrical signals and chemical signals.

The neuron is a cell with dendrites, the axon, and the terminal branch. Messages are received by structures called dendrites, and then sent to the cell body in the form of electrical signals. When activated, the neuron carries signals (impulses) to the axon. At the end of the neuron is the terminal branch. This is where the impulse exits the neuron. Only two kinds of signals are possible: excitatory, when they signal "Activate and transmit a message" to the neuron, and inhibitory, when

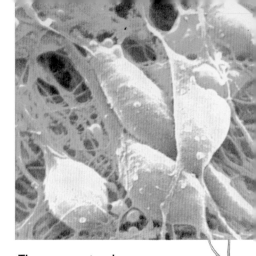

The neuron network
In the brain, many neurons are connected creating an intricate network. In this micro-photo, the cell bodies of several neurons enlarged 400 times can be seen.

Receivers
These molecules are present on the membrane of the interlocutory cell. The message is received when the neurotransmitters link to them.

Between the cells
The space that separates the synapses of the cell that receives the message is extremely narrow, barely 0.2 thousandths of a millimeter.

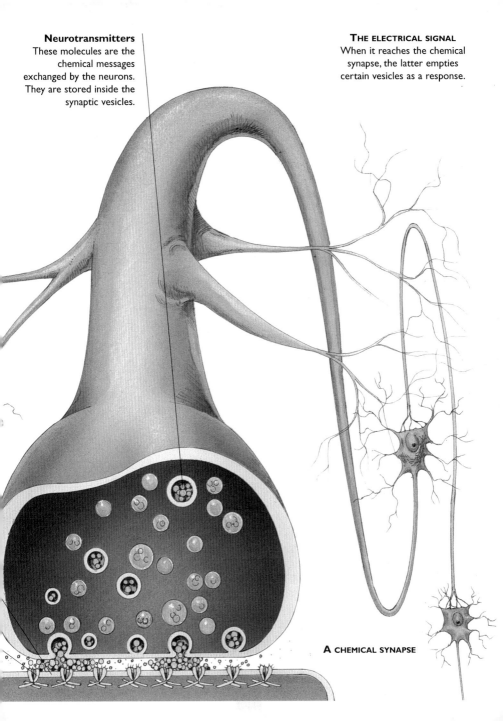

Neurotransmitters
These molecules are the chemical messages exchanged by the neurons. They are stored inside the synaptic vesicles.

A CHEMICAL SYNAPSE

THE EFFECTS OF ALCOHOL
It is truly a drug, creating dependency and, in excessive quantities, causing harmful effects to many organs.

Pain
The neurons that transmit sensations of pain are blocked initially, thus the pain is not felt.

The liver
When it breaks down alcohol, it produces toxic substances that cause nausea and pain.

Drowsiness
Alcohol imitates the action of an inhibiting neurotransmitter called GABA. It creates a sensation of drowsiness. If the quantity of alcohol is so high as to inhibit too many neurons, a person can die.

Vasodilation
The flow of blood to the skin increases, and a sensation of heat is experienced. But it is illusory because the blood, running near the surface, chills, and the body temperature lowers.

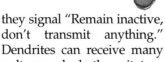

they signal "Remain inactive, don't transmit anything." Dendrites can receive many signals simultaneously, both excitatory and inhibitory, which are then "tallied" in the cell body. If the former prevail, the neuron is activated and generates an electrical signal, which travels on the axon until it reaches its terminus.

The terminal branch is in contact with other cells, which are often nervous or muscular cells or belong to a gland. The message is directed toward them, and the muscle will contract or the gland will secrete a hormone. In rare cases, the electrical signal passes directly from the neuron to its interlocutor by means of button-like structures called electrical

COMPARING BRAINS
The human brain is very different from
that of other animals, although all brains
are made up of neurons.

The human brain
has a lot of gray matter, or
cortex. The higher functions,
such as thinking, come from
activity that takes place here.

The monkey
Its DNA is very
similar to a human's,
and the chimpanzee's
is actually 99%
identical. However,
the few remaining
genes are enough to
make it a very
different brain.

A dog's brain
doesn't have much cortex, but
the olfactory area is much more
developed than in a human.
Sniffing rather than thinking was
much more important in the
evolution of the dog.

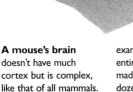

A mouse's brain
doesn't have much
cortex but is complex,
like that of all mammals.
In simpler animals (for

example, the squid) the
entire nervous system is
made up of only a few
dozen neurons.

synapses. This transmission method
produces very quick communication,
but it is not the most common. Rather,
in most neurons, the electrical impulse
is transformed into a chemical signal
when it reaches the axons by other
structures. These are gaps called chemical synapses.

In response, the interlocutor cell

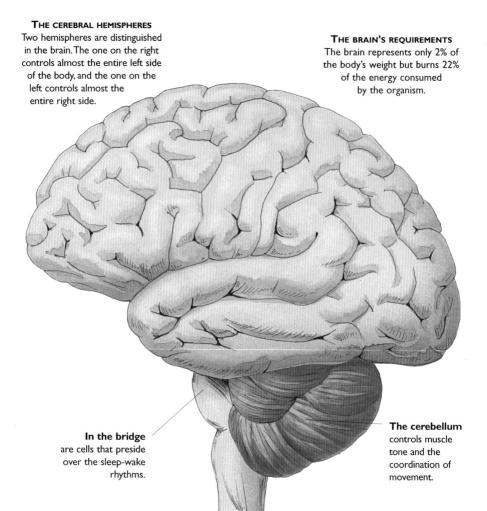

THE BRAIN'S REQUIREMENTS
The brain represents only 2% of the body's weight but burns 22% of the energy consumed by the organism.

In the bridge
are cells that preside over the sleep-wake rhythms.

The cerebellum
controls muscle tone and the coordination of movement.

generates an electrical signal, contracts, or secretes hormones, depending on whether the cell is a nerve, muscle, or glandular cell. There are about 30 known chemical signals, and each neuron generally carries one or two kinds. The transformation of an electrical message to a chemical one enables a highly articulated information system to function.

The Brain

Our brain contains about 100 billion neurons, divided primarily into two sectors: the cortex (where the more complex mental processes and the conscious part of cerebral activity take place) and several structures located under the cortex. The medulla oblongata, a part of the brain stem, is responsible for basic and involuntary

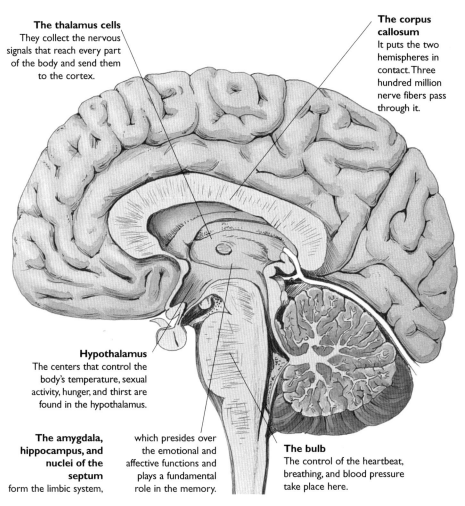

The thalamus cells
They collect the nervous signals that reach every part of the body and send them to the cortex.

The corpus callosum
It puts the two hemispheres in contact. Three hundred million nerve fibers pass through it.

Hypothalamus
The centers that control the body's temperature, sexual activity, hunger, and thirst are found in the hypothalamus.

The amygdala, hippocampus, and nuclei of the septum
form the limbic system, which presides over the emotional and affective functions and plays a fundamental role in the memory.

The bulb
The control of the heartbeat, breathing, and blood pressure take place here.

functions, such as heartbeat. The cerebellum is responsible for coordination, and the limbic system regulates emotion. Reflexes are controlled in both the spinal cord and the brain itself. There is a strict correlation and continuous exchange of information between these structures and the cortex. The most surprising aspect of the cerebral cortex is its plasticity.

The thousands of billions of connections that unite its neurons are not stable, but change continually. When we see a picture, remember a person, or express a concept, a shift occurs in the connections—or synapses—of our brains. As a result, separated neurons link, or they link more tightly so that the transmission of messages becomes simpler. At the same time, other synapses weaken and thus lessen the communication channels that were previously active.

The connections between neurons are what enable us to reason. This means that to be "intelligent," it is more important to have a lot of connections than a lot of neurons. An increase in stimuli increases the number of synapses per neuron. This suggests that the secret to sharpening the brain's mental capacities is to keep it active and to exert oneself to understand and study new things.

Although the brain maintains its plasticity throughout its life, its capacity to change is at it maximum during the first years of development. In that period, groups of neurons "decide" what their tasks will be: whether they will preside over language, memory, hearing, or any other function. This came to light when it was accidentally discovered that when a very young child's eye was bandaged (for example, because of wound), he would lose the ability to see in that eye. This happened because the neurons that transmit the visual images to the cortex did not receive any stimulus for several weeks and thus abandoned the closed eye and specialized instead in another function. Once these cells took another path, they could not return to their previous function, and the eye remained unable to see, although all of its parts were functioning perfectly. It is somewhat like having a functional light bulb that has been disconnected from a house's electrical system.

The ear
perceives sounds produced by music and sends corresponding stimuli to the cortex cells. They examine the sounds and in several fractions of a second are "aware" if they correspond to the piece of music that has been learned.

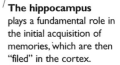

The hippocampus
plays a fundamental role in the initial acquisition of memories, which are then "filed" in the cortex.

The fingers
It is difficult to move them quickly and in a precise order. However, training makes the movements natural because the connections between the neurons relative to a certain sequence are strengthened, which are then activated in succession without uncertainty or errors.

Sleeping in phases
Sleep has two different phases, called synchronized sleep and REM (Rapid Eye Movement) sleep, the latter characterized by rapid eye movements behind the lowered eyelids. These two phases follow a regular cycle of about 90 minutes, in which only 10–15 are REM and the rest synchronized. It is in this last phase that the body moves, changing position (about 10 times per night), while dreams occur during REM.

Light sleep

REM stages

Heavy sleep

1   2

SLEEP
About one-third of our life is spent sleeping, but it is not yet clear why it is so important. According to some scientists, when we sleep the memories that are formed in the course of the day are transmitted to the cortex, where they are filed definitively.

Sleeping and waking
Sleeping and waking alternate, like the different phases of sleep, owing to the neurons of the bridge, which send signals (inhibitory or excitatory, respectively) to the cerebral cortex.

Communication with the torso and limbs

The brain does not exchange information directly with the arms, legs, and organs. The messages that it receives and transmits pass through the neurons of the spinal marrow first, which, together with the brain, make up the central nervous system. The nerves branch off from the spinal marrow, located in the spinal column, and represent the peripheral nervous system. They carry the nerve stimuli from the central nervous system to the peripheral organs and vice versa. The peripheral nervous system is divided into somatic and autonomous (or vegetative): the first transports information from the sense organs to the central nervous system and regulates voluntary movements, while the second regulates those functions of the body that are not controlled by the will. The neurons of the cells that make up the peripheral nervous system are found in the spinal marrow, or in the adjacent "ganglia," while their axons, joined and wrapped in an insulating layer of myelin, form the white "cords" that we recognize as nerves.

There are two kinds of neurons in the nervous system: sensory and motor. Sensory neurons are made up of axons that carry the impulses picked

THE AUTONOMOUS NERVOUS SYSTEM
is part of the peripheral nervous system and is divided into orthosympathetic and parasympathetic. The former responds to emergency situations with reactions of anger or fear, while the latter presides over rest and recovery of strength.

During anger
1) The orthosympathetic causes the pupil to dilate and salivation to be inhibited. The heartbeat increases and the bronchi dilate to allow more air to enter. In addition, it causes the muscles of the urinary bladder to be released.

Controlling temperature
is one of the extremely important tasks of the autonomous nervous system, which does so mainly by regulating sweating.

During anger
2) Adrenaline and other stress hormones are also produced. Sugar reserves are mobilized in the liver, in order to have energy available, and functions such as the production of gastric juices and sexual activity are inhibited.

up by the peripheral nerves from external receptors. Motor neurons transmit the impulses in the opposite direction, that is, from the central nervous system to the muscles and glands.

Not all actions are determined by the brain. The human body can also undergo involuntary reactions called reflexes. These are generally very quick

During relaxation
1) The parasympathetic causes the pupil to contract and salivation to be activated. The heartbeat slows down and the bronchi constrict because little oxygen is needed. The muscles of the urinary bladder contract.

During relaxation
2) Stress hormones are not produced, the liver accumulates sugars, while the production of gastric juices increases, and the sexual organs are stimulated.

movements. For example, if you touch a boiling surface, the impulse for pain travels through a sensory neuron or nerve fiber and reaches the spinal cord. From there, the stimulus of a motor neuron or fiber departs immediately, which assures that the finger muscles pull back. In this way, one moves away quickly from the source of danger, saving even the small amount of time it would take the brain to become aware of what was happening and to send a message to move the hand. In fact, we are aware of what has happened only when the movement has already been completed, and then we feel the pain.

Relationships with the outside
The brain continually analyzes information coming from the outside world

Waking up

When we sleep, our eyelids are closed and the oxygen from the air doesn't reach the cornea (which coats the eye and is the only part of the body that also receives oxygen directly from the outside). As a result, an emergency mechanism is activated to draw energy without oxygen. In this way, however, lactic acid is produced, accumulating in the cornea and causing it to swell and be less efficient.

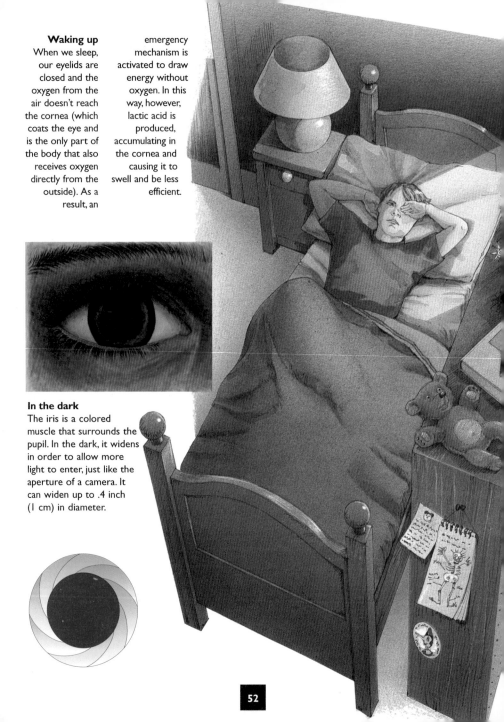

In the dark

The iris is a colored muscle that surrounds the pupil. In the dark, it widens in order to allow more light to enter, just like the aperture of a camera. It can widen up to .4 inch (1 cm) in diameter.

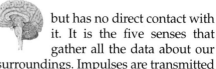

In the light
The iris contracts up to .05 inch (1.5 mm), in order to prevent the retina from receiving too much light. The dilation of the iris doesn't necessarily depend on the light, but can be prompted by anger, fear, or drugs.

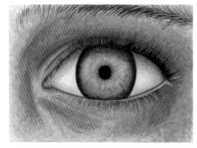

Processing information
The brain is not limited to registering information from the outside. It also processes and interprets it. For example, it is very easy for a person to recognize that this object is a bottle, even if it is partially hidden. This is because the brain, owing to its experience, also reconstructs the invisible part of the image. This operation is extremely difficult even for the most sophisticated computer.

but has no direct contact with it. It is the five senses that gather all the data about our surroundings. Impulses are transmitted to the brain through sensory neurons. On the basis of this information, the brain constructs an image of the environment that is sufficiently precise to enable a person to live in it.

Thus, an object or phenomenon is real to us only if we can see, hear, touch, smell, or taste it. Or, rather, it is real only if our senses can pick up a signal about its existence. Therefore, the information that reaches the brain is information selected from the outside world that will enhance our chances for survival. We cannot pick up ultrasound, as can bats, or see infrared, as can certain insects, simply because for millions of years the brain of our species has had no basic need to receive this kind of information.

It is as if the environment that surrounds us were a building with dozens of rooms, but we have the keys to enter only five of them, because those five are the zones in which we find comfort.

Sight

Sight is considered the most important of our senses. In fact, three-quarters of our perceptions are visual or are influenced by what we see. Sometimes we need only to watch the snow falling to feel a cold chill, and a beautiful fruit can seem more aromatic than it really is compared to a less attractive piece. Reflecting their importance, the eyes are located inside the head, in the most protected spot of the organism.

The human eye can see only objects

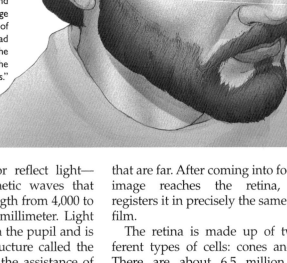

PROCESSING IMAGES
The image of an object, captured by the eyes, is transformed into nervous signals and transmitted to the cortex.

The retina
Its cells react to an image by generating a nervous signal. This is transmitted to the cortex by the neurons of the two optic nerves.

The optic nerves
The nerve fibers from the internal part of each retina intersect in the optic chiasma and head toward opposite directions of the cortex. This intersection helps the brain to create three-dimensional images.

The striated cortex
creates a preliminary recognition of the shapes and colors of objects, but the image is completed in other zones of the brain. A knock to the head can excite the neurons of the striated cortex, causing the impression of "seeing stars."

that emit or reflect light—electromagnetic waves that range in length from 4,000 to 7,000 millionths of a millimeter. Light enters the eye through the pupil and is focused by a lens structure called the crystalline lens. With the assistance of several small muscles in the eye, the structure curves to focus on objects that are near, or flattens to observe those are far. After coming into focus, the image reaches the retina, which registers it in precisely the same way as film.

The retina is made up of two different types of cells: cones and rods. There are about 6.5 million cones, which specialize in seeing color, but they are active only when the light is intense. There are 125 million rods,

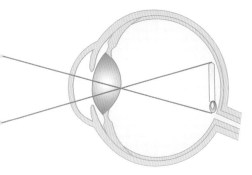

Upside-down images
The crystalline lens functions like the lens of a camera and "projects" upside-down images onto it. The brain then interprets the image and turns it upright.

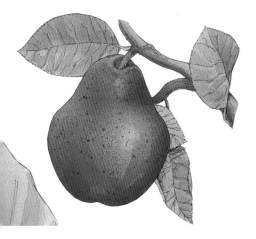

which are sensitive even when the light is dim, but they are not able to recognize color. This is why everything appears in black and white at night.

The rods contain a molecule called rhodopsin, which comes from vitamin A. When rhodopsin is struck by a ray of light, it splits and generates a nervous signal. This signal is transmitted to the neurons of the optic nerve

With a different vision
The outside world can take on very different aspects if it is seen from the eyes of a cat, which can adapt itself to the dark, or an elephant, which can identify the tender buds on which it feeds, or a fish, which can see very wide fields under water.

TRICKS AND TRAPS
The brain has difficulty identifying certain images, which can deceive it.

How many colors?
The central line is the same color, but the brain is deceived by the background and "sees" the top edge as darker.

and, through them, to the brain.

The cones become stimulated as well and transmit their signal to the brain with a mechanism that is similar to that used by the rods. The only difference is that the cones do not contain rhodopsin. Instead, they contain three different molecules that are sensitive to light. One of them splits when it is struck by a red ray, one when the ray is green, and the third when it is blue. All of the gradations that are perceived by the human eye come from the different combinations of these three primary colors. The majority of people can distinguish 150–200 colors, but there are exceptions. For example,

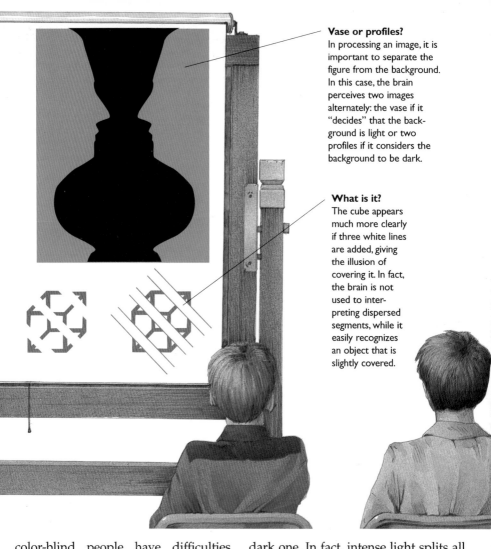

Vase or profiles?
In processing an image, it is important to separate the figure from the background. In this case, the brain perceives two images alternately: the vase if it "decides" that the background is light or two profiles if it considers the background to be dark.

What is it?
The cube appears much more clearly if three white lines are added, giving the illusion of covering it. In fact, the brain is not used to interpreting dispersed segments, while it easily recognizes an object that is slightly covered.

color-blind people have difficulties distinguishing certain hues because they do not have enough cones that are sensitive to green and blue light.

Given that photosensitive molecules split when they are struck by light, they have to be resynthesized continually. This phenomenon is evident when we go from a very bright place to a very dark one. In fact, intense light splits all of the photosensitive molecules in the rods. Coming into a dark setting, we do not see anything initially because the available molecules in the rods have been used up, and the light is not sufficient to activate the cones. As time passes, however, the photosensitive molecules form again, the rods function

The cochlea
is a small tube
1.4 inches (35 mm)
long that makes up
the internal ear.

**The semi-circular
canals**
Like the cochlea, they are
filled with liquid. They
form the vestibule and
preside over the sense
of balance.

The acoustic nerve
transmits the stimuli
registered in the
cochlea to the brain.

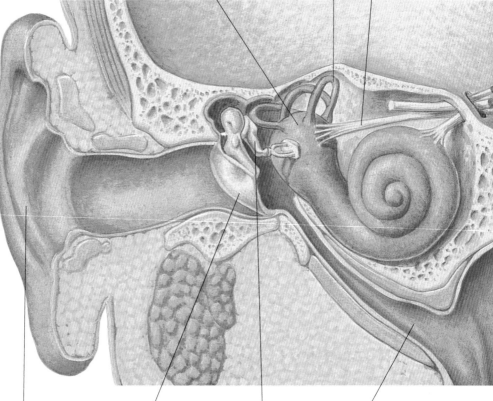

The external ear
collects sounds and
conveys them toward
the eardrum.

The eardrum
is a membrane about
.4 inch (1 cm) thick.
Its level of tension can
be modified by the ear-
drum's tensor muscle,
which makes it more or
less sensitive to sound
vibrations.

The middle ear
is comprised of the
malleus, the incus, and
the stapes.

The eustachian tube
A cold can obstruct the
nasal extremity. In this
case, the pressure of the
two sides of the eardrum
vary, causing a lowering of
the hearing which remains
until the balance is
restored.

Decibels

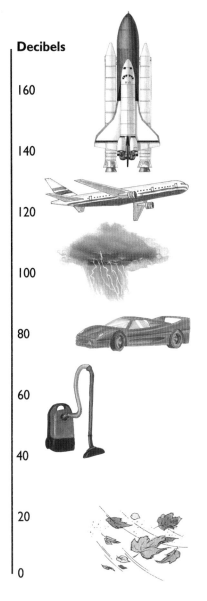

160

140

120

100

80

60

40

20

0

What we hear
The intensity of sounds is defined in decibels. The value of 0 decibels has been given to the minimum sound that a person can perceive. On the other hand, sounds that are above 140 decibels are so strong that the eardrum can break.

 once more, and objects become recognizable.

Hearing

Sounds are vibrations of particles produced by objects in motion in the air. The human ear perceives them when their frequency, or the number of vibrations per interval of time, is between 20 and 20,000 hertz. All of the sounds that a person needs to hear for survival purposes are in this interval: those produced by predators, by a fallen object, and by the human voice, which has a frequency of several hundred hertz. Other animals have different needs, and their ears can perceive different wavelengths. For example, elephants communicate by emitting low-frequency sounds that we are unable to hear, but that they can understand very well. In the same way, bats emit and recognize ultrasounds with frequencies of about 50,000 hertz.

With hearing, people need to perceive sounds, to pick up external stimuli, and to transform them into nervous signals. To achieve this, the ear is divided into different sections, each with a different function. The external ear collects sounds and conveys them toward the eardrum. This is a membrane that vibrates when it is struck by sound waves, and the intensity of the vibration varies according to the length of the wave. For the eardrum to function, the air pressure must be equal on both sides. This is done by the eustachian tube, located behind the eardrum. The tube is about 1.5 inches (4 cm) long, and its other end is in the pharynx. The vibrations produced by the eardrum cause the movement of three ossicles, the malleus, the incus, and the stapes, which strike against the cochlea (a scroll-shaped tube that is filled with liquid). These small blows cause the formation of waves in the cochlea's interior, which are transmitted until they reach a zone called the organ of Corti. This is made up of about 15,000 cells, each with about 100 cilia (similar to those in the cells of the respiratory tract). The cilia bend and twist at the passing of the waves, and their movements stimulate the waves to produce a nervous signal that is sent to the brain.

Touch
Touch is a sensation that is perceived through sensory receptors located throughout the body. Tactile sensations serve to inform the brain of the general conditions and needs of the body and can be of three types: pressure, temperature, and pain. The sensations are picked up by nerve endings in the skin, at various levels of depth. These endings have different kinds of structures, according to the sensation that they are specialized in receiving and the impulses they are transmitting to the brain. They can end freely in the epidermis, in contact with tactile cells, or be wrapped in special structures called Meissner, Pacinian, Ruffini, and Kraus corpuscles. Not every zone of the body has an equal concentration of each kind of ending. As a result, some parts receive sensations of pain very well while others are more sensitive to temperature or touch. For example, the eye's

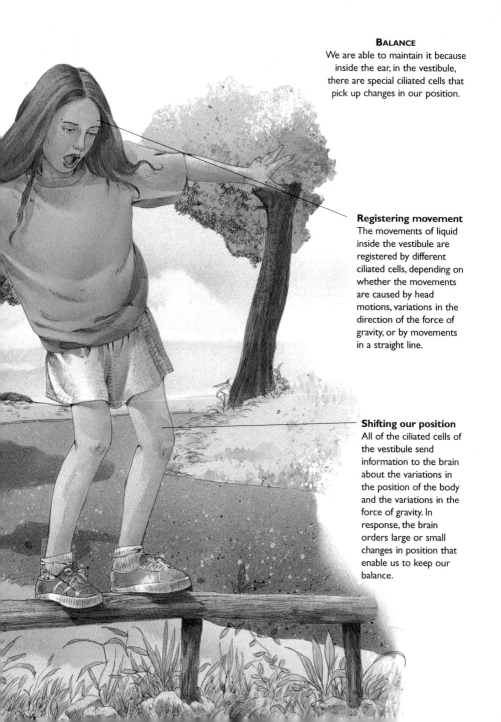

BALANCE
We are able to maintain it because inside the ear, in the vestibule, there are special ciliated cells that pick up changes in our position.

Registering movement
The movements of liquid inside the vestibule are registered by different ciliated cells, depending on whether the movements are caused by head motions, variations in the direction of the force of gravity, or by movements in a straight line.

Shifting our position
All of the ciliated cells of the vestibule send information to the brain about the variations in the position of the body and the variations in the force of gravity. In response, the brain orders large or small changes in position that enable us to keep our balance.

ANSWERING A QUESTION
Even if this is banal, many parts of
the brain need to be activated,
beginning with the auditory part.

The question goes from the
auditory area to Wernicke's area,
which structures
the response.

"What's your name?"

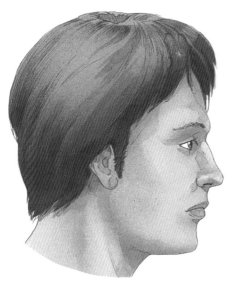

Hearing area

From Wernicke's area
the signals cross the arched fascicle and pass
to Broca's area, which communicates to the
motorial area the order in which to move one's
lips and pronounce the response. If Broca's area
is damaged, one can still "think" the response
but cannot articulate its sounds.

cornea is very sensitive to
pain but not to touch.

Taste

Being able to distinguish edible foods
from poisonous ones is a fundamental
need for the survival of a human being
and is achieved primarily through
taste. Tastes are received by about 3,000
structures, called taste buds, located on
the tongue. The sensations of sweet,
salty, sour, and bitter are recognized by
different taste buds located in specific
zones of the tongue. Every other taste is
a combination of some or all of these
four.

Taste is perceived by numerous receptors on the tongue. The action of saliva is necessary because food particles
must be moistened before they can flow

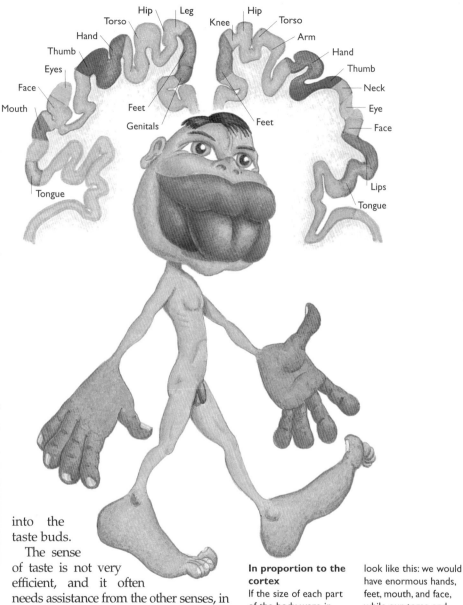

In proportion to the cortex

If the size of each part of the body were in proportion to the zone of the cortex with which it exchanges information, we would look like this: we would have enormous hands, feet, mouth, and face, while our torso and limbs, which are not very sensitive to touch, would be much smaller.

into the taste buds.

The sense of taste is not very efficient, and it often needs assistance from the other senses, in particular sight and smell. For example, if you are blindfolded and your nose is closed, it is not easy to distinguish the taste of orange juice from grapefruit juice.

Smell

The sense of smell is located in the nose and, like taste, serves to inform the body of the quality of the food swallowed, but also to transmit pleasant or unpleasant sensations about the objects in the surrounding environment. Before a person can perceive odors from something, molecules or small particles must diffuse through the air and be inhaled by the nose. In the upper part of the nose, there are special cells called olfactory cells that latch onto the molecule with tiny cilia. At the same time, they send a signal to the brain, which identifies it with a certain odor. The human sense of smell is able to recognize up to 10,000 different odors. Sometimes, in order to heighten the sense of smell, a person takes a deep breath, which increases the number of molecules that reach the cilia of the olfactory cells.

The sense of smell is often lost for brief periods. For example, it happens when we have a cold, because the abundant secretions of nasal mucus prevent air from reaching the olfactory cells. The infection destroys cells that are needed wto detect odors. Too, the sense of smell may be altered under certain conditions. During pregnancy, certain odors that were once pleasant suddenly become repulsive.

The endocrine system

The body doesn't always respond to information from the external environment, picked up by the nervous system, with a simple and immediate

The free nerve endings generally receive pain stimuli, but some are sensitive to touch.

Tactile cells register sensations of touch and send them to nearby free nerve endings.

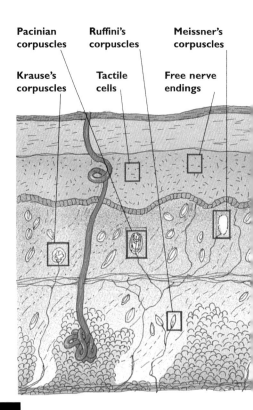

| Pacinian corpuscles | Ruffini's corpuscles | Meissner's corpuscles |
| Krause's corpuscles | Tactile cells | Free nerve endings |

Pacinian corpuscles
are sensitive to pressure. They are made of a nerve fiber ending, immersed in a gelatinous substance, and enclosed in a thin concentric wrapping. They are about one-third of an inch wide.

Ruffini's corpuscles
Are sensitive to heat. They have a spindle-like structure enclosed in a nerve ending divided into several branches. They are from .008 to .08 of an inch (0.2 to 2 mm) long.

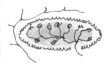

Meissner's corpuscles
are sensitive to touch. They are made of a wrapping that contains a nerve ending, divided into different branches. They are about 40–50 thousandths of a millimeter long.

Krause's corpuscles
are sensitive to cold. They are similar to Pacinian corpuscles but are rounder and smaller.

TACTILE ILLUSION
Like all the senses, the sense of touch can also be tricked. Holding an object in two crossed fingers, and not looking at it, one can easily believe that one is touching two different objects situated on the sides of the fingers.

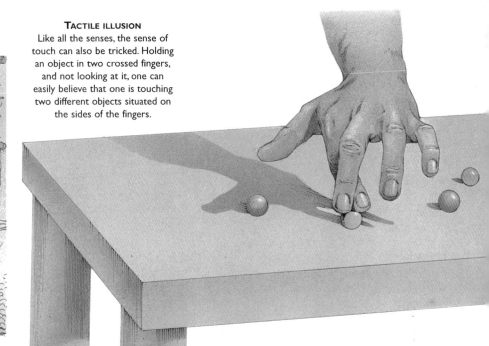

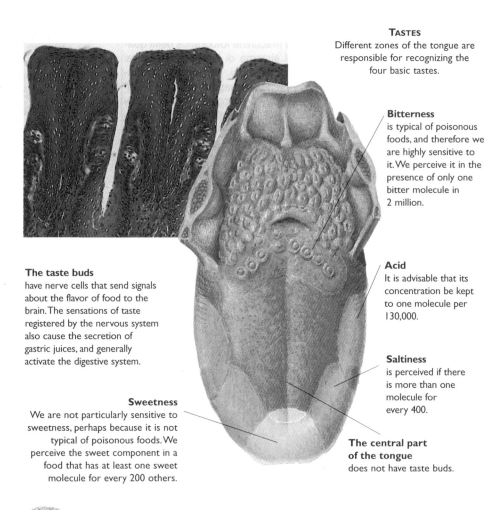

TASTES
Different zones of the tongue are responsible for recognizing the four basic tastes.

Bitterness
is typical of poisonous foods, and therefore we are highly sensitive to it. We perceive it in the presence of only one bitter molecule in 2 million.

The taste buds
have nerve cells that send signals about the flavor of food to the brain. The sensations of taste registered by the nervous system also cause the secretion of gastric juices, and generally activate the digestive system.

Acid
It is advisable that its concentration be kept to one molecule per 130,000.

Saltiness
is perceived if there is more than one molecule for every 400.

Sweetness
We are not particularly sensitive to sweetness, perhaps because it is not typical of poisonous foods. We perceive the sweet component in a food that has at least one sweet molecule for every 200 others.

The central part of the tongue
does not have taste buds.

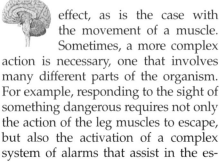

effect, as is the case with the movement of a muscle. Sometimes, a more complex action is necessary, one that involves many different parts of the organism. For example, responding to the sight of something dangerous requires not only the action of the leg muscles to escape, but also the activation of a complex system of alarms that assist in the escape. Such an overall mobilization cannot be achieved through direct stimuli, such as the usual ones of the nerve cells; thus, it is carried out by the hormonal system. This system also guarantees communication among all the internal organs, so as to coordinate the physiological processes that take place without our being aware of it. We have already seen insulin and glucagon,

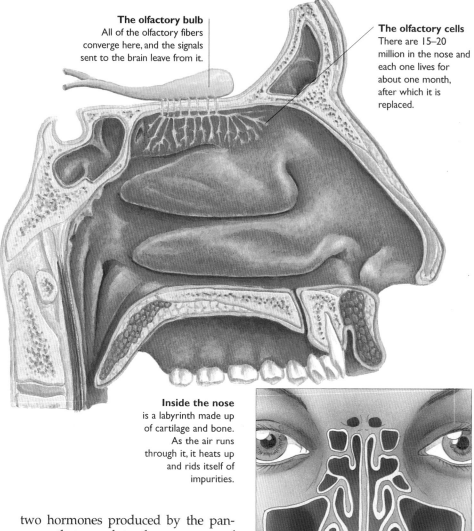

The olfactory bulb
All of the olfactory fibers converge here, and the signals sent to the brain leave from it.

The olfactory cells
There are 15–20 million in the nose and each one lives for about one month, after which it is replaced.

Inside the nose
is a labyrinth made up of cartilage and bone. As the air runs through it, it heats up and rids itself of impurities.

two hormones produced by the pancreas that regulate the presence of sugar in the blood and consequently play an important role in the hunger and satiety stimuli. On the other hand, the coordination of processes that have broader effects (for example, growth, development, and reproduction) depends upon hormones of different systems. In molecular terms, hormones are primarily lipids or proteins. They are produced by a system of glands, called endocrine, that pours them directly into the blood. The hormones are transported throughout the organism and are picked up by those cells that have the appropriate receptor on their membrane—a molecule that fits perfectly with the hormone. Each hormone has its specific receptor.

The endocrine glands act under the strict control of the nervous system, in particular the zone of the brain called the hypothalamus. Information related

THE MAIN GLANDS

In their entirety, they weigh only 5.3 ounces (150 g) but they greatly influence the entire organism. It takes less than one hormone molecule for every million molecules in the blood to produce significant effects.

The pineal gland produces melatonin, a hormone that regulates the sleep-wake cycle and influences the development of the sexual organs.

The pancreas produces insulin and glucagon, two hormones that regulate the presence of sugars in the blood.

Ovaries

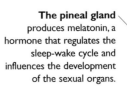

Endocrine gland	Exocrine gland	Cell	Blood vessel

Hormones

Different glands

There are two types of glands: endocrine and exocrine. The former secrete hormones, pouring them into the blood vessels, while the latter release their products outside the organism or in the organs where they must act. Examples of exocrine glands are sweat and salivary.

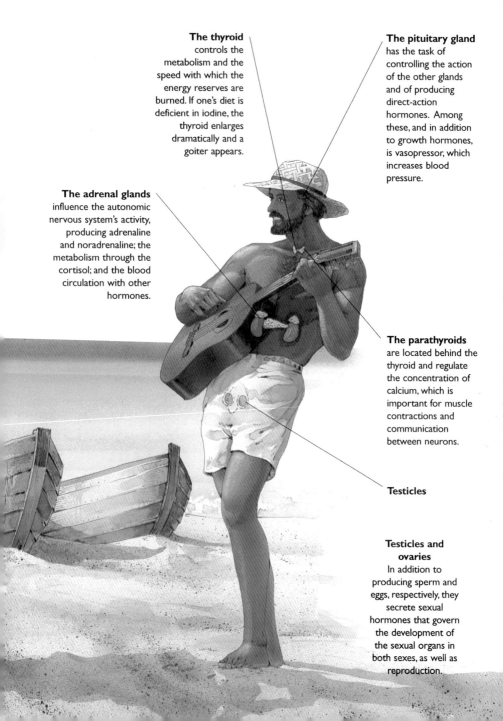

The thyroid controls the metabolism and the speed with which the energy reserves are burned. If one's diet is deficient in iodine, the thyroid enlarges dramatically and a goiter appears.

The pituitary gland has the task of controlling the action of the other glands and of producing direct-action hormones. Among these, and in addition to growth hormones, is vasopressor, which increases blood pressure.

The adrenal glands influence the autonomic nervous system's activity, producing adrenaline and noradrenaline; the metabolism through the cortisol; and the blood circulation with other hormones.

The parathyroids are located behind the thyroid and regulate the concentration of calcium, which is important for muscle contractions and communication between neurons.

Testicles

Testicles and ovaries In addition to producing sperm and eggs, respectively, they secrete sexual hormones that govern the development of the sexual organs in both sexes, as well as reproduction.

to the external environment and the internal conditions of the organism continually converge here from the other parts of the nervous system. In response, the hypothalamus sends stimuli to the pituitary gland, a gland that is as large as a pea and serves as the hormonal system's "orchestra conductor." To perform this function, the pituitary gland secretes hormones directly to the other endocrine glands, which are then inhibited from or stimulated to produce their hormones. In addition, the pituitary gland secretes other hormones that are able to act directly on certain processes, such as the body's growth. Because of its many influences on the cells in the body, the pituitary gland is termed the "master gland."

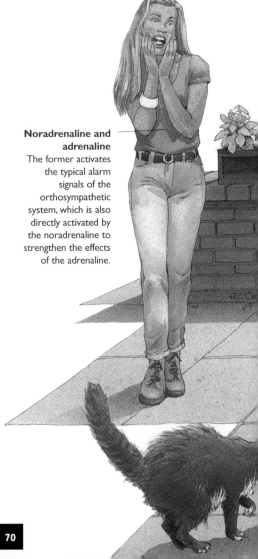

the organism needs to alert all parts of the body quickly and simultaneously. Thus, it chooses to communicate through a hormone, adrenaline—produced by the adrenal glands together with noradrenaline.

Noradrenaline and adrenaline
The former activates the typical alarm signals of the orthosympathetic system, which is also directly activated by the noradrenaline to strengthen the effects of the adrenaline.

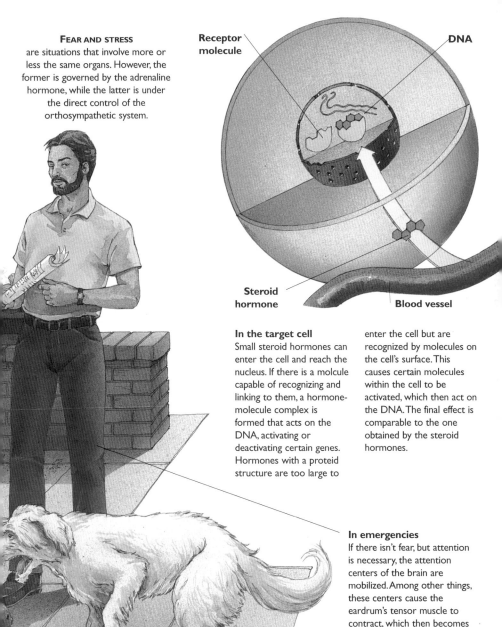

are situations that involve more or
less the same organs. However, the
former is governed by the adrenaline
hormone, while the latter is under
the direct control of the
orthosympathetic system.

**Receptor
molecule**

DNA

**Steroid
hormone**

Blood vessel

In the target cell

Small steroid hormones can
enter the cell and reach the
nucleus. If there is a molcule
capable of recognizing and
linking to them, a hormone-
molecule complex is
formed that acts on the
DNA, activating or
deactivating certain genes.
Hormones with a proteid
structure are too large to
enter the cell but are
recognized by molecules on
the cell's surface. This
causes certain molecules
within the cell to be
activated, which then act on
the DNA. The final effect is
comparable to the one
obtained by the steroid
hormones.

In emergencies

If there isn't fear, but attention
is necessary, the attention
centers of the brain are
mobilized. Among other things,
these centers cause the
eardrum's tensor muscle to
contract, which then becomes
more sensitive.

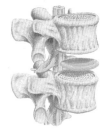

THE HUMAN BODY IN MOTION

A human being is recognized immediately because of its shape. That it moves shows that it is alive and in action. Both the body's shape and movement are products of the bones and muscles.

The problem of holding oneself up

The skeleton is the framework of the human body, and it is also the base to which the muscles are attached. The lever system on which the muscles act to cause movement is in fact similar to a working machine. Moreover, the bones in the skeleton enclose and protect the more delicate organs. The skeletal system stores such minerals as calcium. Hormones influence the release of this mineral when the body needs it in the blood. Another

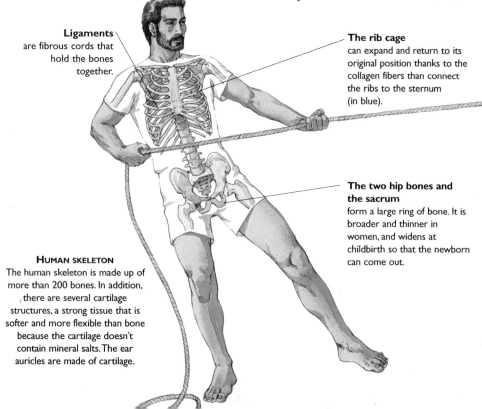

Ligaments
are fibrous cords that hold the bones together.

The rib cage
can expand and return to its original position thanks to the collagen fibers than connect the ribs to the sternum (in blue).

The two hip bones and the sacrum
form a large ring of bone. It is broader and thinner in women, and widens at childbirth so that the newborn can come out.

HUMAN SKELETON
The human skeleton is made up of more than 200 bones. In addition, there are several cartilage structures, a strong tissue that is softer and more flexible than bone because the cartilage doesn't contain mineral salts. The ear auricles are made of cartilage.

important function of bones is the production of blood cells.

The most surprising aspect of the bones, however, is their extraordinary mechanical properties. They are among the strongest materials in existence: one cubic centimeter of bone can support 1,100 pounds (500 kg). At the same time, they are flexible—as is shown by their resistance to blows and falls—and very light. The average weight of an adult skel-eton is 20 pounds (9 kg), which is four times less than it would weigh if it were made of steel. Its resistance to weight and to blows comes from its structure, which is an interweaving of different components. About 65 percent of bone is calcium and phosphorous salts. This is the hard part of the bone. Collagen fibers are interspersed. Collagen is an elastic substance that enables the bones to remain intact even if twisted to a certain degree.

MUSCLES
The body moves because of about 600 muscles consciously controlled by the brain. Added to these are the muscles that enable the internal organs and the heart to contract, which are involuntary movements.

Pectoral muscles
are developed in width.

The limb muscles
Like the arm biceps, they are developed in length.

SHORT MUSCLES
surround the eyes and the body's orifices. Short muscles of very different shapes are also found around the joints and the spinal column.

Tendons
are fibrous bands that anchor the muscles to the bone, allowing the connection between the skeleton and the muscular apparatus.

The tissues around the broken femur swell. In this way, more nutrients and oxygen reach the traumatized zone to repair it. In addition, the swollen and painful leg is a continual signal that serves as a reminder to avoid other accidents.

The only thing that surgeons can do is to join the two bone ends and wait for them to heal by themselves. In this case, one has recourse to a special support in which the external part of the leg is also used.

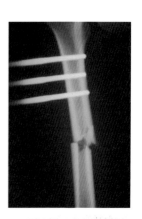

BREAKING IN THE RIGHT SPOT

Bones are structured so as to break in the thinnest spot when subjected to excessive pressure. In this way, the blow is absorbed and doesn't strike in other parts of the skeleton, where it could cause more serious damage.

Pain

As soon as the accident occurs, the brain receives signals from the neurons near the bone, and the transmission of sensations of pain weakens for several minutes. In this way, the victim isn't paralyzed by the pain and can move away if danger should persist.

The osteoblasts that were in the bone before the break multiply; only 8 hours after the fracture, they have begun reconstruction work. A month after the accident the healing is already well along.

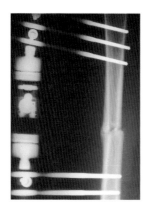

Five months after the accident, the bone is perfectly repaired, but the part that has been reconstructed is slightly thicker than normal. In the following months, thanks to the work of the osteoclasts, the bone will return to its optimal shape.

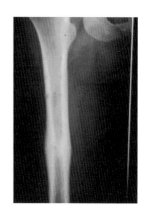

The skeleton's rigidity might make us think of it as dead tissue. This is not the case. Rather, it renews itself constantly. Besides collagen and mineral salts, there are two kinds of cells: osteoclasts, which continually destroy and reabsorb the older bone sections, and osteoblasts, which rebuild them. Bones thus re-form nonstop. Those points subject to the most tension are continually strengthened. For example, the feet of classical ballet dancers take on a different shape that enables the body to hold itself on its tiptoes. Similarly, the skeleton of an astronaut weakens in space because of the lack of force normally imposed by gravity, and quickly returns to normal when the astronaut returns to earth. If the body has a calcium deficiency, the osteoclasts intensify their work to release greater quantities of this mineral and make it available to the other cells. Thus, the calcium in the bones is a reserve for the entire body. This reserve is replenished by the osteoblasts as quickly as possible, after it is depleted.

In elderly people, however, bone formation drops off in general. Hormonal changes in men and women result in a further drop in bone replacement. This can result in a condition called osteoporosis in which the bones are much more fragile than normal.

To allow the osteoblasts and osteoclasts to be replaced, the bones are crossed by a network of blood vessels located in tiny channels. Inside the ribs, vertebrae, pelvis, and skull bones is the red marrow, where all blood cells are produced. The bones along the limbs contain yellow marrow, primarily adipose tissue, an emergency reserve of energy used when body fat has already been burned.

How we move

The skeleton's rigid framework consists of a lever system that moves under the action of about 600 voluntary muscles anchored to the bones by cords of tissue called tendons. Normally, they represent 23 percent of a woman's body weight and 40 percent of a man's.

Running to each voluntary muscle are nerves that originate in the spinal cord. They become active only when stimulated. These nerves can be influenced by the areas of the brain that govern voluntary action. Most movements by adults—walking or picking up an object—occur so often that people do them automatically. Consequently, they are generally performed unconsciously, without the involvement of the areas of the brain that are responsible for reflecting on how

THE LIFE OF BONES
In an adult, about 10% of each bone is replaced each year. In the elderly, the process is slower, but even at 95 years of age there is no part of the skeleton that is more than 20 years old.

After birth
Initially, the skeleton of the fetus is made up of cartilage, which is gradually replaced by real bone. The process begins at two months gestation. Even after birth, the bones have certain cartilage areas, which are their points of growth and disappear when growth is completed.

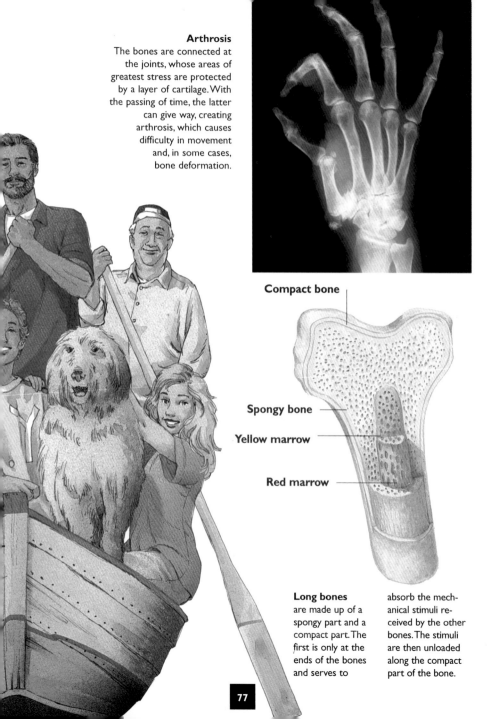

Arthrosis
The bones are connected at the joints, whose areas of greatest stress are protected by a layer of cartilage. With the passing of time, the latter can give way, creating arthrosis, which causes difficulty in movement and, in some cases, bone deformation.

Compact bone

Spongy bone

Yellow marrow

Red marrow

Long bones are made up of a spongy part and a compact part. The first is only at the ends of the bones and serves to absorb the mechanical stimuli received by the other bones. The stimuli are then unloaded along the compact part of the bone.

JOINTS

The majority of bones can move with respect to the others thanks to mobile joints. In order to reduce friction, they are wrapped in a sleeve of smooth tissue that is filled with a lubricating liquid, similar to the way the parts of a motor work.

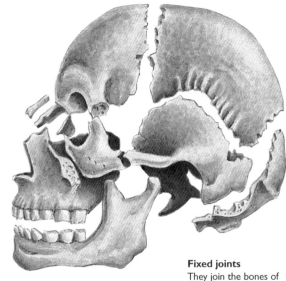

Fixed joints
They join the bones of the skull, which are not mobile.

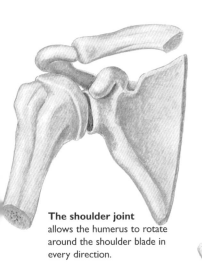

The shoulder joint
allows the humerus to rotate around the shoulder blade in every direction.

Vertebrae
are separated by a disk of cartilage that reduces friction between them. Their front part is the body's central axis, and the rear part houses and protects the neurons of the spinal cord.

The knee
Its joint enables the tibia to bend on the femur in one direction.

and when to perform them. This is not innate, but acquired in the first years of life.

The cells of the voluntary muscles are indistinct, merged to form structures called muscular fibers: they are fixed in number at birth and do not increase with exercise. Exercise alters the size of each fiber and so causes

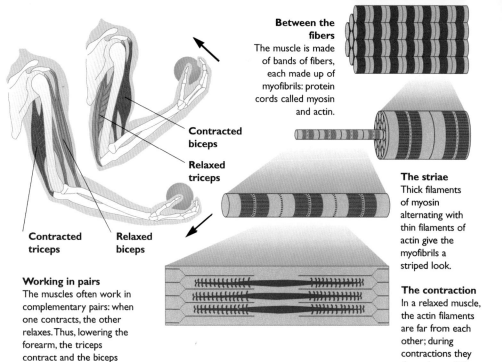

Between the fibers

The muscle is made of bands of fibers, each made up of myofibrils: protein cords called myosin and actin.

The striae

Thick filaments of myosin alternating with thin filaments of actin give the myofibrils a striped look.

Working in pairs

The muscles often work in complementary pairs: when one contracts, the other relaxes. Thus, lowering the forearm, the triceps contract and the biceps relax; the opposite takes place when the forearm is raised.

Contracted biceps

Relaxed triceps

Contracted triceps

Relaxed biceps

The contraction

In a relaxed muscle, the actin filaments are far from each other; during contractions they draw closer, sliding onto the myosin filaments.

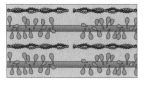

Energy for the muscle

A series of "small hooks" are on the myosin filaments, and during the contraction they link and slowly draw near the action filaments. ATP is needed for this operation.

muscle size to increase. Another characteristic of voluntary muscles that change with exercise is their resistance to exertion. In fact, there are two types of fibers: red and white. The former are able to remain active for a long time and without interruption, while the latter can withstand intense but brief exertions. With regular exercise, our muscles become able to stay active longer because the white fibers are partly converted into red ones.

To contract naturally, muscles need energy, which they draw from their reserve of ATP, produced through cellular respiration. With overly intense exertion, however, cells may not take in enough oxygen for the cellular respiration to take place. The result is that an emergency mechanism is activated, which enables ATP to be produced in the absence of oxygen, although in smaller quantities. Lactic acid is produced as a waste molecule in this process. Because it is acidic, it causes pain as it accumulates in the muscles.

With prolonged exertion, however, the muscles deplete their reserves and become temporarily rigid, producing cramps. Massage is one method used to restore function; it encourages an influx of new nutrients into the blood as well as the removal of lactic acid. Lactic acid is sent to the liver, which converts it into sugars, activating a chemical reaction that requires oxygen. The body restores its oxygen supply through deep and intense breathing that continues even after physical exertion has ended.

In addition to voluntary muscles, the body has other muscles, which are linked to fibers of the autonomic nervous system. These muscles cannot be consciously controlled. They are smooth muscles, which coat the internal organs and blood vessels, and the cardiac muscle, found only in the heart. They do not consist of

THE CARDIAC MUSCLE
is very strong and can contract steadily for our entire life. As we grow older, however, the risk of heart damage increases greatly, in particular of a heart attack. Other factors that contribute to this illness are a sedentary life, fatty foods, stress, and smoking.

Exertion
The volume of air pumped by the lungs increases as much as 20 times, and the heartbeat can go from 70 to 120 beats per minute.

CHOLESTEROL
Plates of fat, called cholesterol, form in the blood vessels. They grow larger as we grow older. If the blood flow is very fast, one of these plates can break; a blood clot is created around it which obstructs the blood vessel.

Myocardial infarction (heart attack)
occurs when the artery that serves the heart is obstructed. In this case, the cardiac cells no longer receive oxygen and begin to die.

fibers, like voluntary muscles, but are composed of distinct cells. Smooth muscles also function differently from voluntary muscles. The former have weak, slow, long contractions, which are required, for example, to propel food through the digestive tract. The latter can contract quickly or slowly, for a long or a short time, depending on the need.

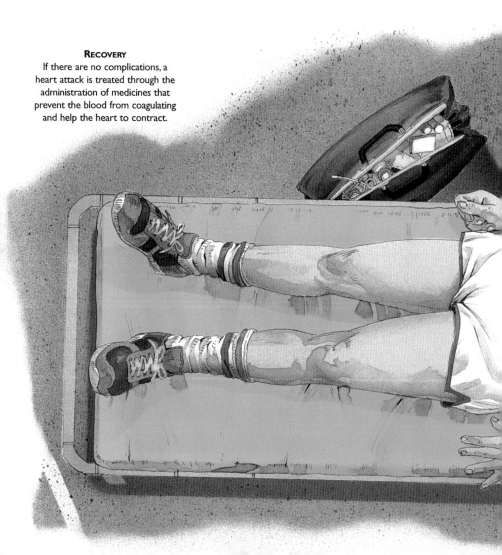

RECOVERY
If there are no complications, a heart attack is treated through the administration of medicines that prevent the blood from coagulating and help the heart to contract.

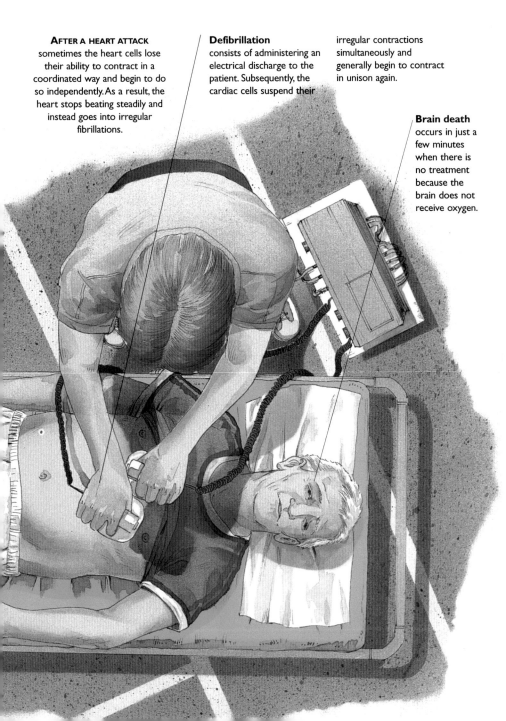

AFTER A HEART ATTACK sometimes the heart cells lose their ability to contract in a coordinated way and begin to do so independently. As a result, the heart stops beating steadily and instead goes into irregular fibrillations.

Defibrillation consists of administering an electrical discharge to the patient. Subsequently, the cardiac cells suspend their irregular contractions simultaneously and generally begin to contract in unison again.

Brain death occurs in just a few minutes when there is no treatment because the brain does not receive oxygen.

THE HUMAN BODY DEFENDS ITSELF

For the human body to survive and function properly, it is not enough that each one of its parts is constantly supplied with what it needs. The entire system must also know how to defend itself from danger in its own environment.

The true enemies of the human species are not large predators, which we have learned long ago how to render less harmful. We continue, however, to battle billions of bacteria and viruses. These may penetrate and attack the body from within, causing diseases that harm us by destroying cells or producing toxins that poison cells.

The skin is the body's first line of defense. This tissue offers a protective barrier from pathogens. Some openings, however, are necessary to permit air and food to enter and excrement to leave the body, as well as the eyes, the ears, and the genitals. These entrances are defended by various mechanisms and traps. Thus saliva, nasal secretions,

THE HAIR serves to protect the head from the danger of excessive heat or cold. In its evolution, hair has also acquired an important role in sexual attraction.

Wavy hair has an oval section.

Straight hair has a round section.

Curly hair has a square section.

tears, and urine contain lysozyme, a molecule that kills many bacteria. The area of the female genitals is made acidic and unwelcome to pathogens by the presence of lactic acid. The acids in the stomach and in the small intestine make life difficult for the pathogens that have worked their way into the digestive tract. Any bacteria that may reach the large intestine will compete with the "good" bacteria living there, and can hardly win a place among them. As we have seen, the mucus covering the inside of the respiratory tract traps any enemies that venture in, while the movement of the eyelashes keeps them away from the eyes. Coughing and sneezing are other ways

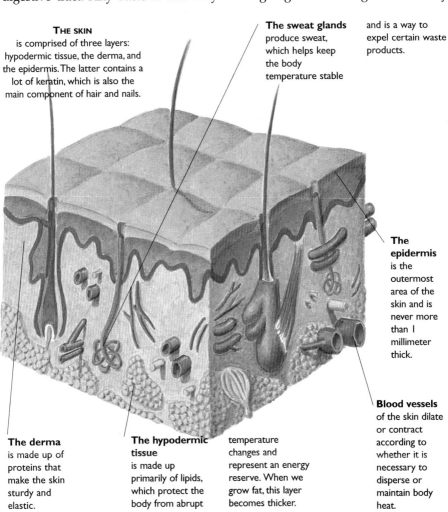

THE SKIN is comprised of three layers: hypodermic tissue, the derma, and the epidermis. The latter contains a lot of keratin, which is also the main component of hair and nails.

The sweat glands produce sweat, which helps keep the body temperature stable and is a way to expel certain waste products.

The epidermis is the outermost area of the skin and is never more than 1 millimeter thick.

Blood vessels of the skin dilate or contract according to whether it is necessary to disperse or maintain body heat.

The derma is made up of proteins that make the skin sturdy and elastic.

The hypodermic tissue is made up primarily of lipids, which protect the body from abrupt temperature changes and represent an energy reserve. When we grow fat, this layer becomes thicker.

Skin color hues
are due to variations in the quantity and kind of pigment produced by melanocytes. However, the number of these cells is unrelated to skin color. It amounts to about 1 % of everyone's skin cells.

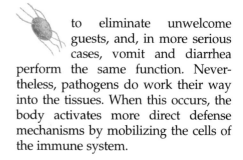

to eliminate unwelcome guests, and, in more serious cases, vomit and diarrhea perform the same function. Nevertheless, pathogens do work their way into the tissues. When this occurs, the body activates more direct defense mechanisms by mobilizing the cells of the immune system.

Ultraviolet rays
are emitted by the sun and trigger a chemical reaction in melanocytes that leads to an increased production of melanin, which is then distributed to all the cells of the epidermis.

The first line of defense: the skin

Covering the entire human body requires about 16 to 22 square feet (1.5–2 sq. m) of skin. This represents 12 percent of a person's total body weight. Its thickness varies: in the eyelids, skin is a few tenths of a millimeter, but on the soles of the feet and in areas that rub against surfaces, it is much thicker.

The skin is composed of many layers of cells. The youngest ones are found in the deep layers and are soft and square. Within days, they are pushed toward the surface by new cells being created underneath, and they become flatter and fill up with a substance called keratin, which makes them tough. The cells of the outermost layers of the skin are dead and full of keratin: they prevent the skin from breaking too easily under strain, even though it is soft and thin. A skin cell lives about one

Too much sun damages skin cells and more nutrients are necessary to repair them. In order to provide these nutrients, the blood flows more abundantly near the skin and makes it red.

SUNTAN
The skin color is partly programmed genetically, but it can become darker if we are exposed to the action of the sun's rays for a long time.

Melanin
Its presence makes the skin more resistant to the sun and protects the DNA from ultraviolet rays. For this reason, fair skin, which contains less melanin, is also the most sensitive skin.

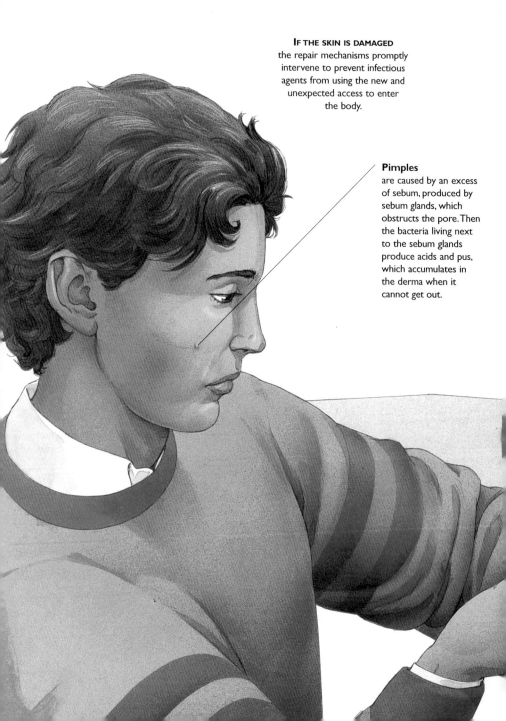

IF THE SKIN IS DAMAGED
the repair mechanisms promptly
intervene to prevent infectious
agents from using the new and
unexpected access to enter
the body.

Pimples
are caused by an excess
of sebum, produced by
sebum glands, which
obstructs the pore. Then
the bacteria living next
to the sebum glands
produce acids and pus,
which accumulates in
the derma when it
cannot get out.

month, and the cells that have reached the outermost layer are constantly shed, a process called desquamation.

The constant turnover of cells of the epidermis makes it difficult for microorganisms to establish themselves on the body's surface. However, it has been calculated that on the skin of a single human, there are about 5 billion organisms, as much as the earth's population. Most of these guests are bacteria or fungi, and they are completely harmless. Every part of the body hosts special types of organisms, and the inhabitants of the forehead's dry skin are as different from those that live in the greasy scalp as a camel is from a polar bear. In the epidermis, one can also find melanocytes, the cells that produce the dark pigment called melanin. This colors the skin and plays an important role in its protection, as it absorbs ultraviolet rays. These rays can damage the DNA in the skin cells and cause cancer.

A wound
The repair process begins with the coagulation of blood, which prevents excessive blood loss and bars the entrance of pathogens. This second goal is more easily achieved if the damaged area is disinfected.

Blood vessel

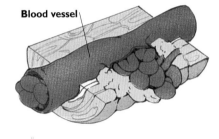

Coagulation
When the skin is wounded, blood platelets go into action. These are fragments of cells called "megacarioblasts," which travel in the blood. They cling to the walls of the blood vessel and, together with another protein called fibrin, they create a clot; that is, a kind of net that also traps some red cells in and "seals" the blood vessel.

Reticulus

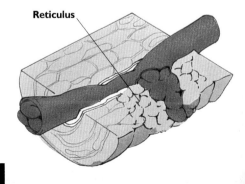

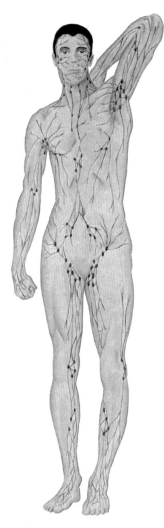

LITTLE ENEMIES

Diseases can be caused by infection from many different kinds of microorganisms and organisms.

Bacteria

Bacteria, such as *Salmonella typhi* (which causes typhoid fever), are primitive forms of life comprised of a single cell. They are highly adaptable, and their main characteristic is that they have no nucleus or organelles, or other specialized structures.

Lymph nodes

are small, rounded organs dispersed along the lymphatic system, and concentrated in the area of the armpits and groin. Lymph nodes produce lymphocytes, blood cells belonging to the white corpuscles and responsible in part for the immune system.

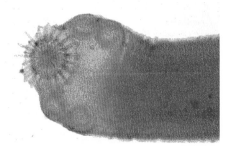

THE LYMPHATIC SYSTEM

plays a fundamental role in the immune system. It is made up of a network of vessels that run throughout the body and of several lymph nodes. Lymph flows in the vessels, which run into the bloodstream. Lymph is a liquid that enters between the tissue cells and transports nutrients and collects waste, even from cells that are not directly touched by the bloodstream.

Worms

Many of them infect human beings and can invade different organs. Tapeworms settle in the intestines, where they survive by absorbing nutrients ingested by the person. They can grow to be 22.4 feet (7 m) long.

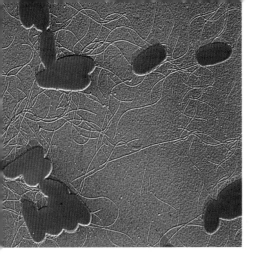

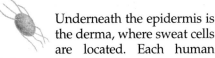 Underneath the epidermis is the derma, where sweat cells are located. Each human being possesses 3 million such cells. On a very warm day they can produce 2 to 3 quarts (or liters) of sweat. The structures that produce hairs are also in the derma. Hairs are found all over the body except on the lips, on the palms of the hands, and on the soles of the feet, but many of them are so thin that they are virtually invisible. They become visible only when it is very cold and they stand up, creating the small bumps that are commonly called "goose bumps." Each hair is connected to two small sebum glands, which secrete an oily substance covering the hair itself and the outer surface of the skin. Sebum helps make the skin soft and retain moisture.

When the enemy penetrates the body
If the pathogens succeed in penetrating the body, the battle becomes harder, for they reproduce very quickly, kill cells, or release toxins that poison them. To prevent the enemies from having the

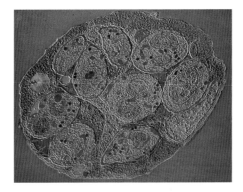

Protozoa are single-cell organisms like bacteria, but their structure is identical to that of human cells: they have a nucleus and several organelles. *Toxoplasma gondii* infects humans, causing toxoplasmosis.

Prions are proteins produced by the system and randomly take on an anomalous shape. Subsequently, they serve as a "mold" and alter all other cells; in the end, they can create dangerous agglomerations. The anomalous protein may be taken in when eating. They cause a disease called Creutzfeldt-Jakob disease in humans and "mad cow syndrome" in bovines.

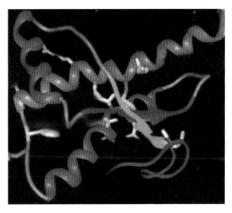

upper hand, the body has at its disposal a very sophisticated defense system: an army of white cells subdivided into highly specialized "troops" that attack the pathogens on more than one front and engage them in close combat.

If the bacteria manage to penetrate a tissue, the damaged cells produce some molecules that act as an alarm system. They first attack the neutrophiles and the macrophages, two kinds of white cells that rush to the site of infection and literally consume the bacteria. These cells can change their own shape to surround the enemy, enclosing it in a blister into which they then pour molecules that destroy it.

Macrophages are constantly patrolling the entire system and also play the role of "street sweepers": besides bacteria, they also eliminate the remains of dead cells or dust particles that have entered the respiratory tract. Following the action of neutrophiles and macrophages, a molecule called histamine is released at the site of infection. Histamine sets off an inflammation; that is, it dilates the blood vessels, allowing more blood, and therefore more white cells, to reach the affected area.

As fast as it may be, the defense enacted by the neutrophiles and macrophages is sometimes not enough. If, for example, the enemy is a worm that is too big for them, other white cells go into action, triggering a chemical defense by secreting substances that destroy the invader's tissues and kill it.

In cases of a viral infection or a more harmful bacterial infection, the human body is compelled to deploy far more

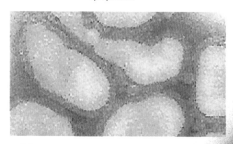

Viruses cause many diseases, including influenza. They are not living beings, but simple protein "boxes" containing a genetic code that enters the infected cells and induces them to produce many copies of the virus.

Fever is typically connected with disease and appears when the mechanisms that regulate temperature are "preset" to a higher temperature than normal. Its usefulness is not yet clear.

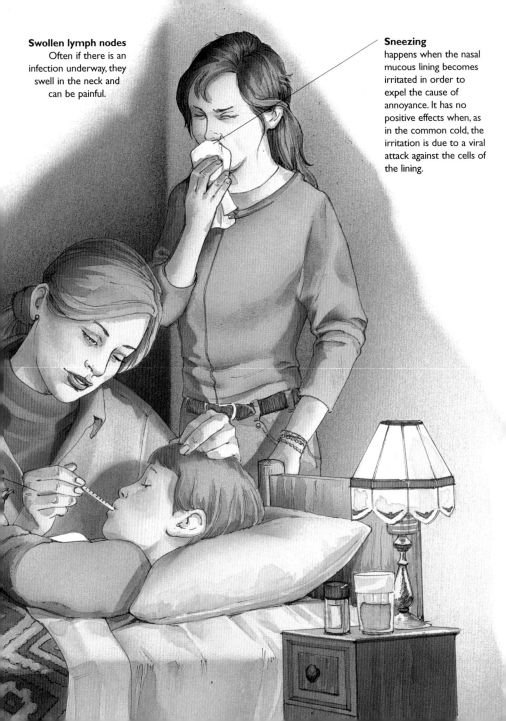

Swollen lymph nodes
Often if there is an infection underway, they swell in the neck and can be painful.

Sneezing
happens when the nasal mucous lining becomes irritated in order to expel the cause of annoyance. It has no positive effects when, as in the common cold, the irritation is due to a viral attack against the cells of the lining.

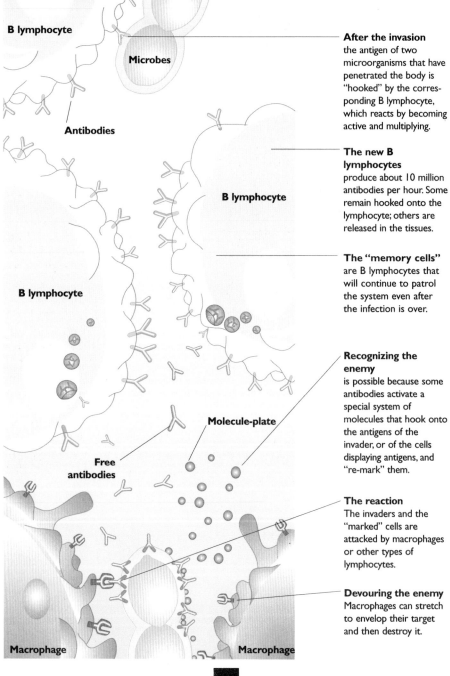

B lymphocyte

Microbes

Antibodies

B lymphocyte

B lymphocyte

Molecule-plate

Free antibodies

Macrophage

Macrophage

After the invasion
the antigen of two microorganisms that have penetrated the body is "hooked" by the corresponding B lymphocyte, which reacts by becoming active and multiplying.

The new B lymphocytes
produce about 10 million antibodies per hour. Some remain hooked onto the lymphocyte; others are released in the tissues.

The "memory cells"
are B lymphocytes that will continue to patrol the system even after the infection is over.

Recognizing the enemy
is possible because some antibodies activate a special system of molecules that hook onto the antigens of the invader, or of the cells displaying antigens, and "re-mark" them.

The reaction
The invaders and the "marked" cells are attacked by macrophages or other types of lymphocytes.

Devouring the enemy
Macrophages can stretch to envelop their target and then destroy it.

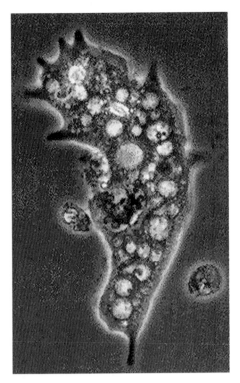

specialized defenses. Viruses have a more specialized way of attacking the body: they multiply within the cells of the host, where neutrophiles and macrophages cannot reach them. In this case, the key to the solution is that every organism or virus is characterized by some molecules that can be recognized as foreign by the immune system. These substances are called antigens. The body has at its disposal at least 10 million cells called B lymphocytes, each one of which can recognize a single antigen. Their number is so high that there exists a type of B lymphocyte for virtually every possible antigen. With a bacterial infection, the antigens circulate in the body, either freely or tethered to the membrane of the macrophages that have previously destroyed the organism they used to belong to. If the infection is viral, the cell that was attacked displays the antigen on its own membrane so as to "warn" the immune system that it is infected. In every case, sooner or later the antigen comes near a B lymphocyte that is able to recognize it. When this happens, the B lymphocyte starts multiplying, creating thou-

Like amoebas
The mechanism by which macrophages and other white cells envelop the bacteria, after sensing their presence with their thin tentacles, is similar to that used by certain single-cell organisms, such as the amoeba, to feed themselves.

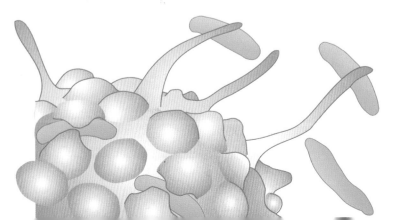

ALLERGIES
The immune system can be activated for common and harmless substances that some B lymphocytes mistake for their antigens. As a result, they multiply as if they had to fight an infectious agent.

Pollen
The most common allergies are caused by proteins present in certain kinds of pollen that are recognized as antigens.

Mites
live in large numbers in mattresses and pillows. Their feces can trigger an allergic reaction.

sands of copies of itself. These copies produce special molecules called antibodies, which are able to bond with the corresponding antigen whether it is on the membrane of a bacteria or is displayed on the membrane of the cell that has been infected by the virus. Subsequently, macrophages and other cells called T lymphocytes recognize and destroy the bacteria or the cell characterized by the antigen-antibody complex.

After the body has fought off the infection, the lymphocytes and most B lymphocytes that took part in the defense die. However, some B lymphocytes stay alive and continue to patrol the system for months, years, or at

The effects of the allergy
The eyes and nose easily come into contact with the antigen. In this case, the B lymphocytes in their tissues stimulate the release of histamine, and they become red, swollen, and "runny."

Cat and dog hair
can be allergens, as can the saliva.

times, a lifetime. If more organisms like the ones that were defeated attempt another attack, they trigger the immune defense in much less time than on the first occasion. Vaccines function on this principle by providing the body with a small number of antigens that are not connected to the microorganism that can cause a disease. When these anti-gens come in contact with the corresponding B lymphocyte, they alert the immune system, and the vaccinated person does not become sick.

MAKING BABIES

The human body is an extraordinary "machine" that can grow, keep itself active, and repair itself. But the most exceptional feat that it can accomplish is to bring another human being into the world.

Humans have a very strong reproductive drive, and the human body has evolved so that it can create and raise a child successfully. Indeed, all living species on earth invest a great amount of their energies in reproduction. Failure to do so could result in extinction. This has been the fate of countless species despite the reproductive drive. To procreate means passing part of our genes to another person, who in turn will pass them on to his or her offspring.

The production of spermatozoa takes place inside seminiferous tubules, contained in the testicles, in a continuous cycle. This means that, even if 72 days are needed for mature spermatozoa to form, in men, unlike what happens in women, there are always mature sexual cells for procreation. The testicles are endocrine glands that also have the function of producing testosterone, the male sexual hormone.

Spermatozoa When mature, they travel along the seminiferous tubules to the epididimus and reach the seminal vesicles.

The testicles hang outside the body because the maturation of spermatozoa must take place below body temperature.

The penis is formed by a spongy tissue covered by skin. During sexual arousal, blood is pumped into the tissue, increasing the size of the penis and making it stiff.

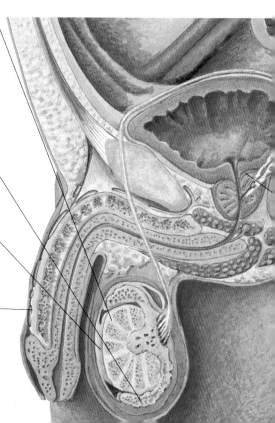

Reproduction ensures that part of us will be able to live on after our death. The human organism has an advantage over other reproducing creatures. The highly specialized brain in humans makes it possible not only for humans to pass genetic material to the next generation, but to pass on cultural heritage as well. Any young *Homo sapiens* born in the Stone Age had the same mental potential as a twenty-first-century child; the latter, however, can use and build far more complex tools than those created by its distant ancestor only because it possesses technological information that human generations have passed on and enriched for millennia.

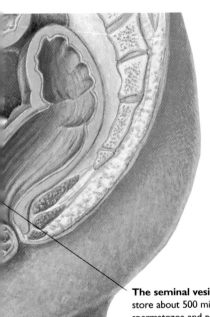

THE MALE REPRODUCTIVE SYSTEM serves to produce spermatozoa and insert them into the woman's body.

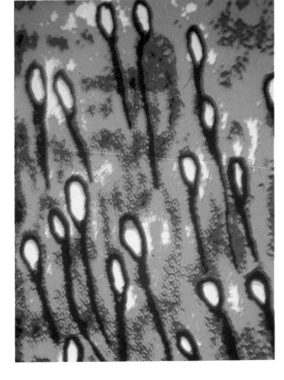

The seminal vesicles store about 500 million spermatozoa and provide the liquid part of the semen. They empty out at the time of ejaculation.

Spermatozoa in motion When mature, the spermatozoa have a tail that helps them move along and makes them resemble microscopic tadpoles. In addition to spermatozoa, semen includes a fluid and nutritious part called seminal plasma.

THE FEMALE REPRODUCTIVE SYSTEM

serves to produce ova and to allow fertilization. Later on, it houses and nourishes the embryo for the 9 months of its development

Fallopian tubes

The ovaries
Here is where the ova mature and then reach the womb after traveling along the fallopian tubes.

Like the testicles, ovaries also function as glands and produce the female sexual hormone called estrogen.

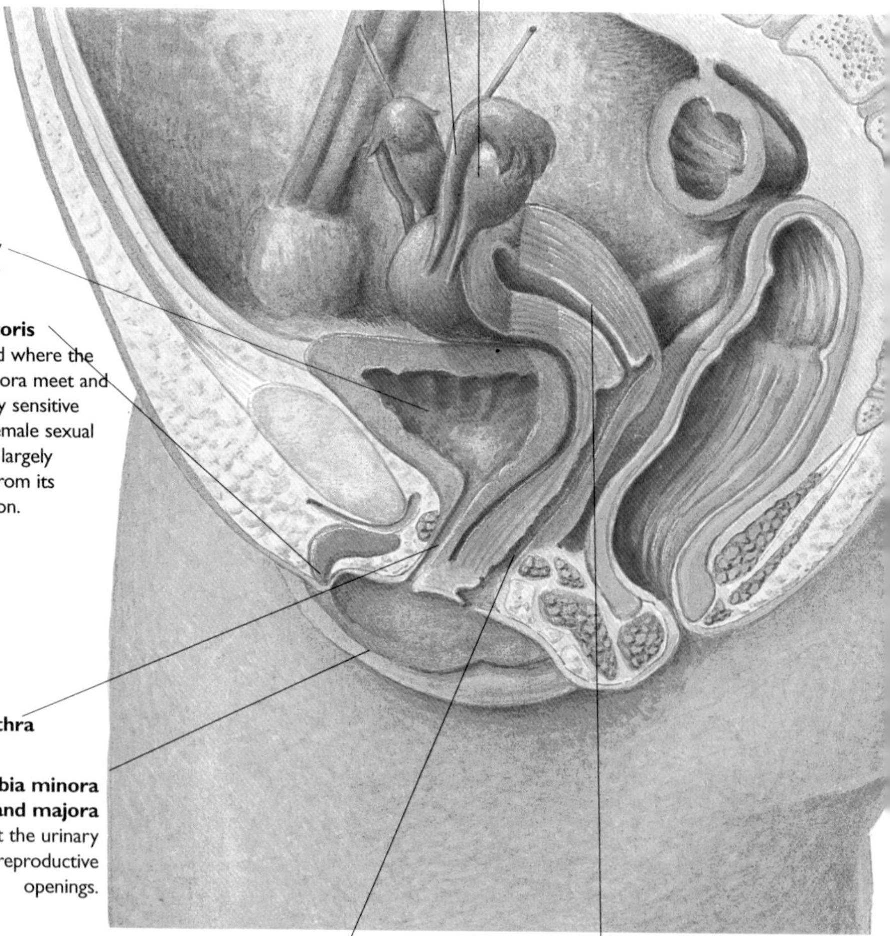

Urinary bladder

The clitoris
is located where the labia minora meet and is a highly sensitive organ. Female sexual pleasure largely derives from its stimulation.

Urethra

The labia minora and majora
protect the urinary and reproductive openings.

The vagina
is located behind the urethra, is about 2.75 inches (7 cm) long and can become very dilated

to receive the penis during intercourse and to allow the baby to exit during childbirth.

The womb (uterus)
has a muscular wall which is 1 inch (2.7 cm) thick and communicates directly with the vagina.

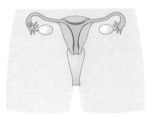
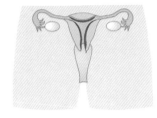
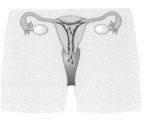

The menstrual cycle
The ovum takes about 14 days to mature in its follicle inside the ovary. Afterward, it is released and travels to the fallopian tubes. For another 14 days, the follicle pro- duces hormones that stimulate the growth of the womb's internal lining, where the fertilized ovum will implant itself. If fertilization does not take place, this lining is expelled with the ovum during menstruation, which lasts about one week; during this time, a new ovum begins to mature. Therefore, a complete cycle—from the beginning of an ovum's maturation to the beginning of the maturation of the next—lasts about 28 days.

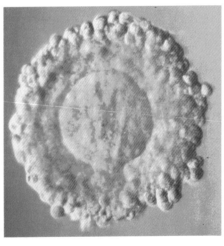

The ova
At birth, a girl's ovaries contain about 600,000 ova, but only 400 of them will mature, at the rate of one per month starting in puberty. Until it implants itself in the womb, the ovum is surrounded by thousands of cells that feed it and protect it.

As with all superior animals, humans reproduce sexually. This means that everyone, male and female, passes on to their offspring only one half of their genetic makeup, while the second half comes from the other parent. For this reason, children resemble both their parents but are identical to neither one. A person's genetic makeup can be imagined as a deck of thousands of cards: every time a child is conceived, the deck is randomly split in two halves and the child receives a copy of one of the halves. However, it is virtually impossible that by halving the deck of cards, one obtains a combination of cards that is identical to the combination obtained by another conception.

For two people to bring a child into the world, their bodies must produce some very special cells, the only ones that do not possess a complete genetic makeup but only one half of the DNA present in all the other cells of their bodies. These cells are the spermatozoa, produced by the man's testicles, and the ova, produced by the woman's ovaries. When an ovum and a spermatozoon merge, the product is called a zygote, that is, the first cell of a new human being. If the reproductive cells possessed the same genetic makeup as all the other cells in the body, the resulting zygote would have twice the amount of DNA as the parents, and this amount would double with each generation.

Men produce new spermatozoa starting at puberty and continue for almost

SEXUAL INTERCOURSE causes an increased frequency of the heartbeat and breathing. It culminates in orgasm, an intense feeling of pleasure that involves the entire body.

Male sexual excitement is manifested by an increased flow of blood into the penis, which grows stiff and can penetrate the woman's body, where it releases the spermatozoa at the end of intercourse, during ejaculation.

Female sexual excitement is less conspicuous than in males and generally includes the secretion by the vagina of a lubricating substance that facilitates penetration by the penis. Reaching orgasm may be more difficult for the woman and it may also take longer.

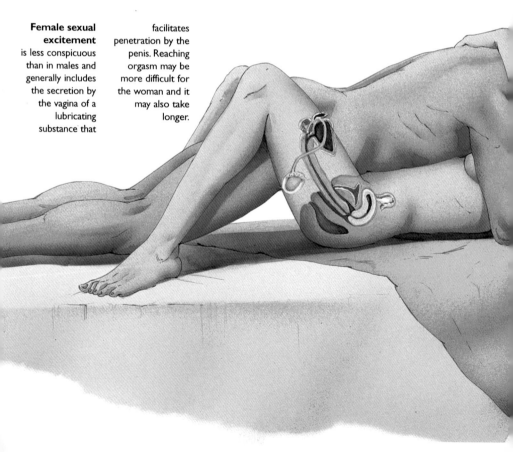

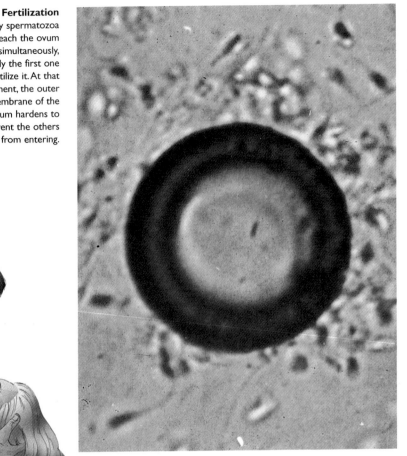

Fertilization
Many spermatozoa reach the ovum almost simultaneously, but only the first one can fertilize it. At that moment, the outer membrane of the ovum hardens to prevent the others from entering.

all their lives. Women, in contrast, produce their ova before birth, but these do not reach maturity immediately. At birth, a baby girl already possesses her final set of ova. They begin to mature at the pace of one every 28 days beginning at puberty and until about 50 years of age. At that age, the activity of the ovaries ceases, and what is called menopause begins.

A new human being arrives

A new life begins at fertilization. At that time, an egg cell and sperm cell unite, and the nuclei are fused. The first cell of the new human being is thus formed, and all other cells will derive from this one. This cell will split millions of times, and the resulting cells will differentiate

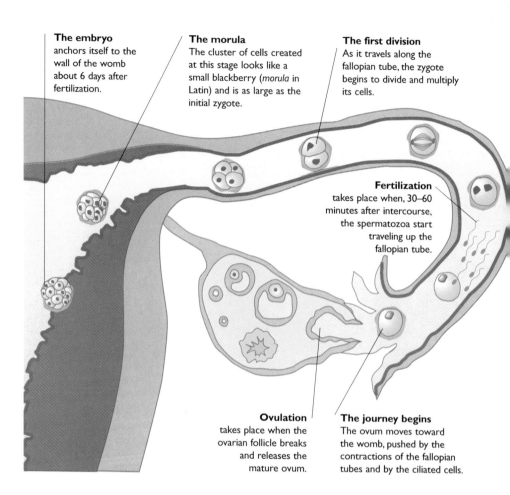

The embryo
anchors itself to the wall of the womb about 6 days after fertilization.

The morula
The cluster of cells created at this stage looks like a small blackberry (*morula* in Latin) and is as large as the initial zygote.

The first division
As it travels along the fallopian tube, the zygote begins to divide and multiply its cells.

Fertilization
takes place when, 30–60 minutes after intercourse, the spermatozoa start traveling up the fallopian tube.

Ovulation
takes place when the ovarian follicle breaks and releases the mature ovum.

The journey begins
The ovum moves toward the womb, pushed by the contractions of the fallopian tubes and by the ciliated cells.

and create all of the different tissues that form the body of a newborn baby, then a child, then an adult, and finally an elderly person. For all this to be possible, an ovum and a spermatozoon must first meet.

This happens as a result of the mating between a man and a woman, during which the spermatozoa are transferred into the female's body. Therefore, the primary natural function of sexual intercourse is to allow reproduction, even if in our species it is often performed for the pleasure it brings and in order to strengthen the emotional ties between two people.

In a woman's body, only one fertile ovum is usually found at a time, and this only for a couple of days each

Identical twins develop from a single fertilized ovum, if at the time of the first cleaving, the cells do not stay together, but separate into two groups which go on multiplying separately. Twins often share the same placenta.

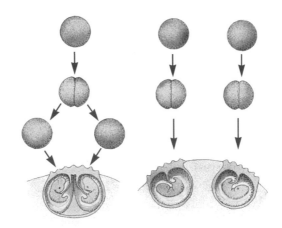

Non-identical twins develop from the fertilization of two different ova that have matured simultaneously. This is very unusual, since ova normally mature one at a time.

The same genetic makeup characterizes identical twins, as they derive from the same ovum fertilized by the same sperm. This explains their perfect physical resemblance.

Different genetic makeup Non-identical twins originate from two different ova fertilized by two different spermatozoa. This is why they only partially resemble one another, like all siblings.

month, when the ovum has just completed its maturation and has been released into the fallopian tubes. During intercourse, a man releases into the woman's body about 500 million spermatozoa, which work their way into the female genitals by moving their "tails" much like tiny fish. Yet only one of them will be able to merge with the ovum. And in order to do so, it must be the fastest in working its way up the vagina, the womb (or uterus), and the entire length of the fallopian tubes. Here, its efforts are rewarded only if sexual intercourse has taken place during the woman's fertile period and a fertile ovum awaits. This journey is so strenuous that most spermatozoa die along the way. At the same time, the difficulty of this enterprise also represents an extraordinary means of selection: there are very few chances that a "defective" spermatozoa will fertilize the ovum before a healthy one does.

Upon reaching the ovum, the spermatozoon breaks its surface and penetrates to the interior. A zygote is thus formed, and no other spermatozoa can merge with the same ovum. Just after fertilization, the newly formed cell begins multiplying, creating first two cells, then four, and so on. About three or four days after fertilization, the embryo, made up of about 16 cells, completes its journey in the fallopian tubes and reaches the womb. Now its main goal is to anchor itself to the mother's body so that it can be nourished and protected during the

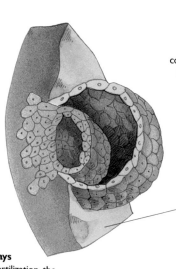

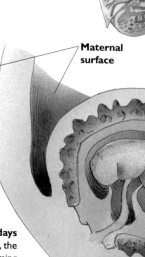

The placenta is a disk-shaped organ, connected to the fetus by the umbilical cord. The mother's and the baby's blood never mix, but they exchange substances through the blood vessels.

Maternal surface

7–8 days after fertilization, the embryo is .04 inch (.1 cm) long and has already anchored itself to the mother's body.

28 days after fertilization, the embryo's head, forming an angle with the body, is already recognizable. The embryo is now .16 inch (.4 cm) long and it has a little "tail" that makes it look like a tiny fish.

months of intrauterine development.

To this end, some of the embryo's cells do not dedicate themselves to forming the baby's body, but instead make up what are called the chorionic villi, which penetrate the walls of the womb as the finger of the hand would into a thick dough. These structures produce a hormone called HCG, which serves to prevent menstruation; other-wise the menstrual blood could wash the embryo away. However, HCG is also responsible for nausea, such as morning sickness, as well as the leth-argy that women experience in early pregnancy. In the following days, the placenta develops on the site where the chorionic villi became implanted in the womb. The placenta is the organ on which the survival of the future human

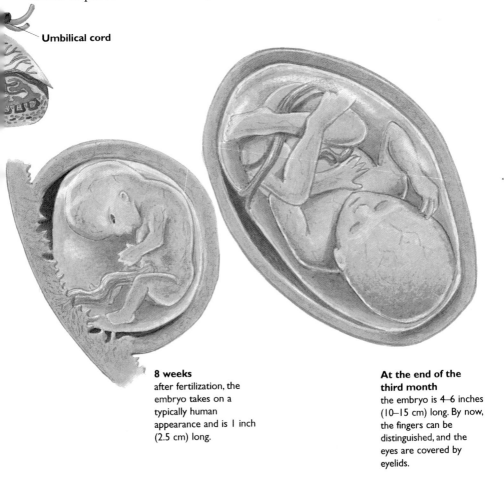

Umbilical cord

8 weeks
after fertilization, the embryo takes on a typically human appearance and is 1 inch (2.5 cm) long.

At the end of the third month
the embryo is 4–6 inches (10–15 cm) long. By now, the fingers can be distinguished, and the eyes are covered by eyelids.

being depends during intrauterine life. It is through the placenta that all exchanges between mother and child take place. It functions like a filter: oxygen and nutrients cross it going from the mother's body to the child; carbon dioxide and other waste that the fetus releases into the woman's bloodstream cross it in the opposite direction. Unfortunately, the placenta may also serve as a channel for infectious agents or substances that can interfere with the baby's development, such as any drugs used by the mother. Other cells derived from the zygote create a sort of sac, called amnion, which envelops the embryo. The sac synthesizes a liquid called the amniotic fluid. The developing baby is completely immersed in it and it protects

AT THE SEVENTH MONTH
the baby is fully developed and could survive even outside the mother's body. The last two months serve to make it stronger and increase its chances of survival after birth.

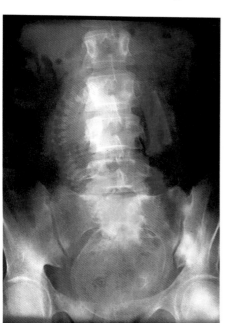

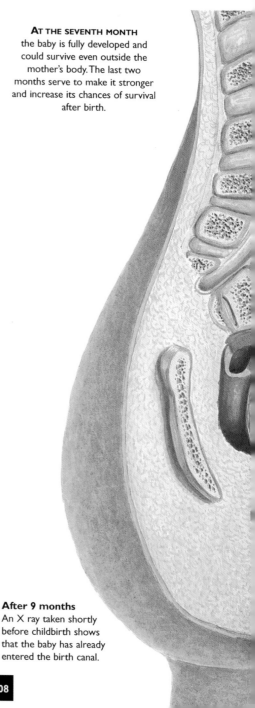

After 9 months
An X ray taken shortly before childbirth shows that the baby has already entered the birth canal.

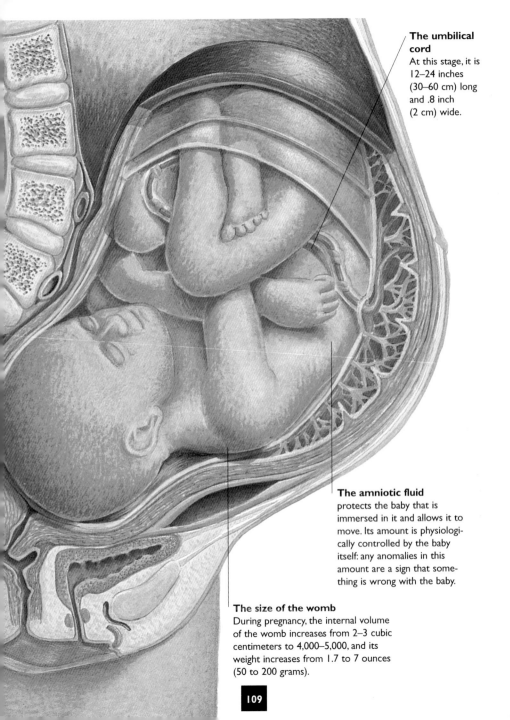

The umbilical cord
At this stage, it is 12–24 inches (30–60 cm) long and .8 inch (2 cm) wide.

The amniotic fluid
protects the baby that is immersed in it and allows it to move. Its amount is physiologically controlled by the baby itself; any anomalies in this amount are a sign that something is wrong with the baby.

The size of the womb
During pregnancy, the internal volume of the womb increases from 2–3 cubic centimeters to 4,000–5,000, and its weight increases from 1.7 to 7 ounces (50 to 200 grams).

the fetus from trauma.

At the end of the ninth week of pregnancy, the fetus already has a typically human appearance. A lot of blood is needed to provide it with the necessary nutrients and oxygen. Therefore, the mother must increase the volume of her body fluids: she often feels thirsty and therefore drinks frequently. Initially, this constant intake of fluids thins her blood, until the woman's body can produce enough red and white blood cells to restore the normal cell concentration. At the end of the third month of pregnancy, the mother's body is perfectly

CHILDBIRTH
begins when the womb's contractions push the baby outside, while the cervix gradually dilates and reaches a diameter of about 3.9 inches (10 cm). 95% of babies come out head first. However, when they are positioned feet first, it may be advisable to perform a surgical operation called Caesarean section.

The baby's skull
The cranial bones of the baby are not fully soldered together: for this reason, as the baby is delivered, the head may become misshapen when passing through the vagina and appear pear-shaped. However, it returns to normal in a short time.

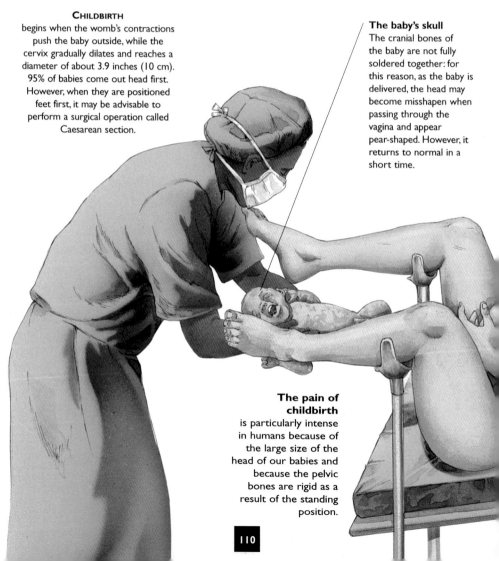

The pain of childbirth
is particularly intense in humans because of the large size of the head of our babies and because the pelvic bones are rigid as a result of the standing position.

equipped to nourish the fetus, and even her physical condition improves, because the nausea and other discomforts typical of early pregnancy subside. The heart, however, is slightly overworked by having to pump an increased amount of blood. At this time, the fetus weighs about 1.05 ounces (30 g); by the end of the pregnancy, it will weigh about 100 times more. In order to make room for the baby, the mother's internal organs progressively shift, and her breasts enlarge as they prepare to produce milk as soon as the baby is born.

A fetus usually takes 40 weeks to

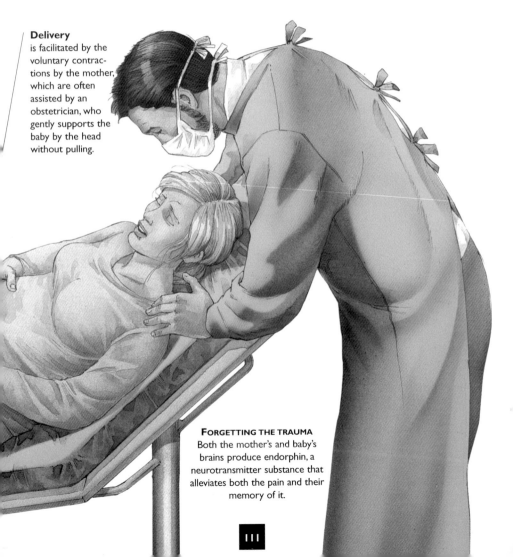

Delivery
is facilitated by the voluntary contractions by the mother, which are often assisted by an obstetrician, who gently supports the baby by the head without pulling.

FORGETTING THE TRAUMA
Both the mother's and baby's brains produce endorphin, a neurotransmitter substance that alleviates both the pain and their memory of it.

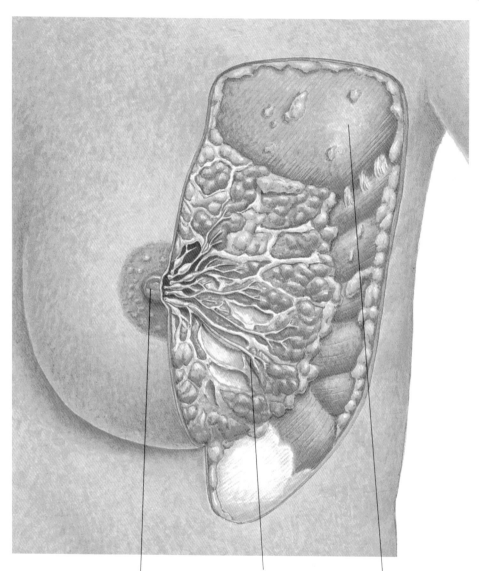

The nipple
About 10–15 milk ducts (galactophores) are located at the nipple. By sucking, the baby triggers nervous signals that stimulate and maintain the production of milk.

Galactophores
are tiny tubes lined with muscular cells that push the milk out when the baby is suckling.

The pectoral muscle
serves to support the breast.

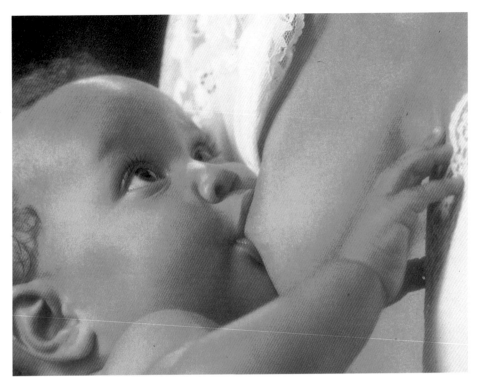

Mother's milk is always at the ideal temperature and contains nutrients in the optimum amount to feed the baby: no other milk can match its qualities.

During breast feeding, the bond between mother and child is strengthened, and the baby receives invaluable psychological stimuli.

Components per liter	A woman's milk	A cow's milk
protein	.4 ounce	1.2 ounces
lactose	2.5 ounces	1.7 ounces
lipids	1.5 ounces	1.3 ounces
mineral salts	.08 ounce	.25 ounce
iron	.5 milligram	.5 milligram
caloric value	700 kilocalories	670 kilocalories

 reach full development, but at 24 weeks it can usually survive outside the mother's body if it is placed in an incubator.

Two or three weeks before childbirth, the fetus usually positions itself with the head down, toward the vagina, where it will leave the mother's body. The birth is heralded by the beginning of labor, when the amniotic sac breaks, and the fluid it contained drains. Then, a series of muscular contractions begins as the muscles of the womb push the fetus outward. The frequency of the contractions increases gradually, but the contractions can go on for as long as 14 hours before they become intense enough to begin the final stage of childbirth, the duration of which varies from a few minutes to many hours.

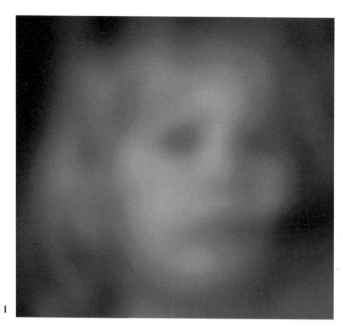

Babies' vision
1) Eyesight is very weak in human babies: when they are a few days old, the main stimuli come from touching, smelling, and tasting. 2) At 3 months, vision has improved but is still weak. 3) At 6 months, images are sharp and the baby begins to form a "mental file" of the surrounding objects.
4) At 8 months, vision is fully developed. In the meantime, the baby has acquired the ability to turn around and crawl on its hands and knees: the time has come to begin exploring the world.

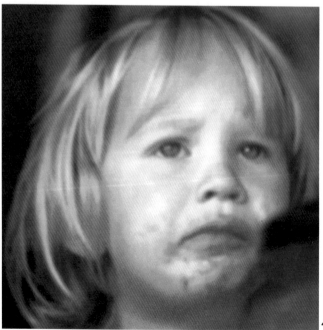

1

2

3

4

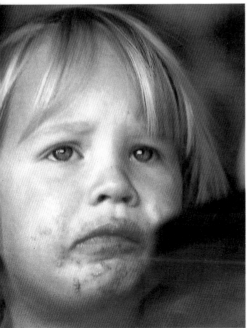

 A baby at birth weighs 7.7 pounds (3.5 kg) on average, is about 19.6 inches (50 cm) long, and is completely unable to survive on its own. Unlike newborns of other species, which can walk only a few minutes after birth and become independent quickly, human babies continue to depend on their parents for a very long time. This is probably one of the reasons for the great success of our species: the long duration of our development, especially that of the brain, gives us a long time to devote ourselves exclusively to learning.

Growing

A newborn baby is extremely weak: the neck muscles cannot even hold up the head. It is also very nearsighted and is unable to identify where sounds are coming from. However, it has some instinctive behaviors, such as sucking the breast when feeding or clutching a finger or any other object placed in its hand. The latter reflex is so strong that the child can suspend itself for a few seconds from a handhold. Furthermore, shortly after birth, if the baby is held in a standing position with just one foot touching the ground, it will instinctively bring the other foot forward as if to take a step. This instinct, however, is lost almost immediately, and even the clutching instinct disappears after the first three months. Walking and clutching are complex actions that will have to be learned again later.

In the first months of life, the baby makes rapid progress, and at 6 months of age it can usually sit up if its back can

lean on something. At around 8 months, most babies begin to crawl, and between 11 months and two years of age, the young human being is already able to walk and express its personality by making its wishes more or less clearly understood. At 6 years of age, the brain has reached 90 percent of its final weight, but many connections between neurons, on which the functioning of the nervous system depends, have yet to be formed. This involves not only the neurons responsible for what is generally called "mental development," but also those

The difficulty of walking
Babies learn to control their muscles from the head down. It is only after they acquire control of their hips and legs that they can begin to walk.

In the early years, the body does not grow uniformly. For instance, at 12 months, the brain has reached half of its adult weight, whereas the rest of the body is much smaller.

The bones
A baby's diet should be rich in calcium because its bones grow very fast.

The thymus is a gland located at the top of the sternum. During childhood, it secretes hormones that are important for growth and the immune system. Around age 14, however, the gland begins shrinking and eventually disappears.

responsible for motion. It is only around age 10 that humans possess the full capacity to understand.

The most delicate and rapid stage of human growth is puberty. This period is characterized by increasing amounts of sexual hormones in the bloodstream, which cause physical and psychological changes. Such changes are often accompanied by a feeling of disorientation and a growing need to become independent and, above all, to define one's identity. Humans continue to grow even after puberty; the growth

Muscular strength
reaches its peak at around 30. Afterward, the muscle fibers begin to die and are replaced by other kinds of tissues.

THE SECOND GREAT TURNING POINT
After puberty, there are no major physical changes in the human body until the end of fertile age.

Puberty
marks the passage from childhood to adulthood. Girls begin to develop the secondary sexual character-istics at around 9 or 10 years of age. At around 12 years, the process is complete, with the onset of the first menstrual cycle.

Full development
is reached between ages 20 and 40, when the body is at the peak of its vigor. There are very few diseases typical of this age, and physical fitness largely depends on adopting a healthy lifestyle.

Between 13 and 15 years
the signs of puberty become evident in young males: the testicles and the penis grow larger, facial hair appears, and the voice becomes deeper.

process continues until around 20 years of age. After that, aging begins, but the physical changes at this stage are so slow that one may not notice them for decades, especially if one adopts a healthy way of life.

Menopause
It usually takes place in women between ages 45 and 55, and marks the end of the fertile period. An analogous event takes place in men, but is not as significant and usually comes later.

Metabolic heat
Elderly people often feel cold because, with the passing of years, some cells in the body die and are not replaced. Therefore, the body misses the heat produced by their metabolism.

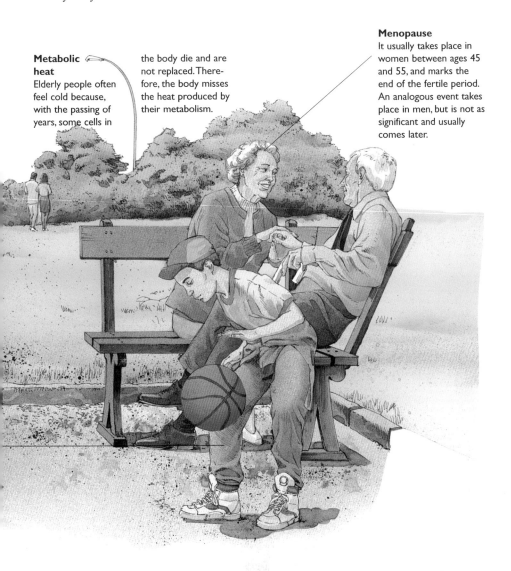

Index

A
Absorption, 19–20
Acidity, 66
Acoustic nerve, 58
Adherent junctions, 7
Adipose cells, 4
Adrenal glands, 69
Adrenalin, 50, 70
Air, purification, 25
Alcohol, 42
Allergies, 96–97
Alveoli, 26–27
Amino acids, 10, 19
Amniotic:
  fluid, 108–109
  sac, 108
Amygdala, 45
Anemia, sickle-cell, 30
Anger, 50
Antibodies, 94–97
Anus, 20
Aorta, 31
Arteries, 33
Arthrosis, 77
ATP, 11–12, 25, 79–80
Atrium, 31–32
Autonomic nervous system, 49–51
Axon, 39, 43, 49

B
Bacteria, 20, 90
Balance, 61
Biceps, 79
Bile, 18
Birth, 110–111
Bitterness, 66
Bladder, 34, 100
Blood, 28, 30
  filtering, 34
  plasma, 30, 33
  red cells, 5, 29, 31
  vessels, 37, 85
Bones, 72–77
  fractures, 74–75
Brain, 44–45
  amygdala, 45
  cells, 11
  cerebellum, 44–45
  comparisons, 43
  corpus callosum, 45
  cortex, 44
  death, 83
  energy requirements, 44
  hemispheres, 44
  hippocampus, 47

hypothalamus, 36, 45, 70
  limbic system, 45
Breast feeding, 113
Breasts, 111–112
Breathing, 24
Bronchi, 25–26
Bronchiole, 25–26
Bulb, 45

C
Caesarean section, 110
Calcium, 9, 72–73, 116
Capillary, 33, 37
Carbon, 9
Carbon dioxide, 25–27
Cardiac muscle, 80
Carnivores, 17
Cartilage, 77
Cell body, 39
Cells, 4–7
  adipose, 4
  blood, 5, 29, 31
  brain, 11
  olfactory, 67
  tactile, 64
  thalamus, 45
Cellular junctions, 7
Cerebellum, 44–45
Cerebral hemispheres, 44
Chemical synapses, 41, 43
Childbirth, 110–111
Cholesterol, 81
Chromosomes, 6–7
Cigarette smoke, 25
Cilia, 25, 60
Circulation, 29–32, 36
Circulatory system, 8
Clitoris, 100
Coagulation, 89
Cochlea, 58, 60
Collagen, 73
Communication, 38–71
Cones, 54–56
Contraction, 79
Coordination, 38–71
Cornea, 62
Corpus callosum, 45
Cortex, 44
Creutzfeldt-Jakob disease, 91
Cytoplasm, 11

D
Decibels, 59
Defibrillation, 83
Dehydration, 36

Delivery, 110–111
Dendrites, 39, 42
Dentine, 15
Derma, 85
Development, 115–119
Diaphragm, 26
Diet, 10
Digestion, 12–25
Digestive:
  system, 5
  tract, 20
DNA, 6–9, 71
Drowsiness, 42
Duodenum, 18

E
Ear, 47, 58–60
  cochlea, 58, 60
  eustachian tube, 58
  semi-circular canals, 58
  stapes, 58, 60
Eardrum, 58
Electrical:
  signals, 41
  synapses, 42–43
Elimination, 32–35
Embryo, 104
Enamel, 15
Endocrine:
  glands, 68–69
  system, 38, 64, 66–71
Endoplasmic reticulum, 7
Endorphin, 111
Energy, 10–37
  brain's, 44
  need for, 12
Enzymes, 18
Epidermis, 85
Epiglottis, 16
Equilibrium, 32–33
Eustachian tube, 58
Exercise, 22–25, 78–79
Exertion, 80
External ear, 58
Eye, 52–53
  cones, 54–56
  cornea, 62
  iris, 52–53
  pupils, 50–51
  retina, 54
  rods, 54–56

F
Fallopian tubes, 100, 105
Fat, 4, 11

Acknowledgments

The illustrations displayed in this volume are new and original. They have been realized upon a project by DoGi s.p.a. that owns its copyright.

ILLUSTRATIONS:
Alessandro Menchi 46-47; Francesco Petracchi 4, 5tr, 13tl, 15t, 20-21, 21b, 26, 27, 28, 31, 34, 39, 48-49t, 52-53, 58, 63, 66, 67t, 78, 85, 90, 98-99, 100-101, 107, 108-109, 112; Silvio Romagnoli 8, 9, 29; Studio Inklink 4-5, 5tl, 5c, 5b, 7, 10-11, 12-13, 14-15, 16, 16-17, 17, 18-19, 20, 21t, 22-23, 24-25, 33, 35, 36-37, 38-39, 40-41, 42, 43, 44, 45, 47, 48-49b, 50-51, 52-53, 54-55, 56-57, 59, 60-61, 62, 64, 65, 67b, 68, 68-69, 70-71, 71, 72-73, 74-75, 76-77, 80-81, 82-83, 84, 86-87, 88-89, 89, 92-93, 96-97, 102-103, 105, 106, 106-107tl, 110-111, 116-117, 118-119.

REPRODUCTIONS AND DOCUMENTS:
DoGi s.p.a. has done its best to discover possible rights of third parties. We apologize for any omissions or mistakes that might have occurred, and we will be pleased to introduce the appropriate corrections in the later editions of this book. Archivio DoGi 25, 30, 31, 40, 66, 86(6), 92, 95; Archivio Isidori-Gallavotti 74, 75, 77; CNRI 91; Farabolafoto 105; Insitut Pasteur/CNRI-Overseas 90-91; Grazia Neri, Milan 103, 108; SIE, Rome 99, 101, 113; Sebastiano Ranchetti 86 (1,2,3,4,5,6)

COMPUTER ARTWORK:
Luca Cascioli 6, 18; Bernardo Mannucci 4, 6-7, 15b, 30, 32, 79, 94; Bernardo Mannucci and Laura Ottina 55tl, 95, 101, 104; Francesco Milo 9; Sebastiano Ranchetti 55tr, 55cr, 55br, 91c, 114, 115

COVER:
Illustrations: Bernardo Mannucci cl; Francesco Petracchi tl, c, cr
Photography: SIE, Romatr
FRONTISPIECE: Studio Inklink

Abbreviations: t: top/b: bottom/ c: center/r: right/l: left.